CALIFORNIA
COOK BOOK

Cooking Across America
Cookbook Collection™

GOLDEN WEST ☼ PUBLISHERS

Front cover photo courtesy of California Avocado Commission
Back cover photos courtesy of Robert Holmes/Cal/Tour

Acknowledgments

Chocolate Soufflé recipe, page 84 from "John Ash One on One: Lessons from a Master Teacher" cookbook published by Clarkson Potter.

Special thanks to the following California produce organizations for their assistance:
Almond Board: www.almondboard.com
Apricot Council: www.califapricot.com
Avocado Commission: www.avocado.org
Cherry Advisory Board: www.calcherry.com
Cling Peach Board: www.calclingpeach.com
Dried Plum Board: www.californiadriedplums.org
Fresh Fig Growers Association: www.calfreshfigs.com
King Salmon Council: www.calkingsalmon.org
Kiwifruit Commission: www.kiwifruit.org
Pear Advisory Board: www.calpear.com
Pistachio Commission: www.pistachios.org
Poultry Federation: www.cpif.org
Raisins Marketing Board: www.calraisins.org
Seafood Council: www-seafood.ucdavis.edu
Strawberry Commission: www.calstrawberry.com
Tomato Commission: www.tomato.org
Walnut Commission: www.walnuts.org

ISBN – 1-885590-67-9

Printed in the United States of America

Golden West Publishers, Inc.
4113 N. Longview Ave.
Phoenix, AZ 85014, USA
(800) 658-5830

For free sample recipes and complete Table of Contents for every Golden West cookbook, visit our website: **goldenwestpublishers.com**

★ ★ ★ ★ *California Cook Book* ★ ★ ★ ★

Table of Contents

Table of Contents (continued)

Introduction

California's culinary history is rich in international influences. From the days of the Spanish missionaries to Gold Rush pioneers and European and Asian immigrants, California foods have been based on traditional specialties enhanced by incredible fresh produce, plentiful and savory seafood, and quality meat and dairy products from farms and ranches.

California cooks prepare favorites that reflect a combination of Old World and New World specialties. California vineyards produce an ever-increasing variety of spectacular wines, perfect accompaniments to many of the dishes presented in this book. The Golden State provides optimum growing conditions for agriculture and California products are shipped worldwide.

Representing the best that California has to offer, *California Cook Book* features recipes contributed by homemakers, chefs, Bed & Breakfasts and agricultural organizations. Prepare these delicious recipes for your family and you're sure to have some new family favorites, too!

California's Produce Capitals!

Many California cities lay claim to being the "Capital of the World."
Visit them and find out for yourself!

Castroville: Artichoke
Fallbrook: Avocado
Fresno: Raisin
Gilroy: Garlic
Greenfield: Broccoli
Half Moon Bay: Pumpkin
Holtville: Carrot
Indio: Date
Isleton: Asparagus
Kelseyville: Pear

Linden: Cherry
Lodi: Tokay Grape
Lompoc: Flower Seed
McCloud: Blackberry
Oakdale: Cowboy
Oxnard: Strawberry
Patterson: Apricot
Plant City: Winter
  Strawberry
Sacramento: Almond

Salinas: Lettuce
Selma: Raisin
Stockton: Asparagus
Tulelake: Horseradish
Watsonville: Strawberry
Yuba City: Prune

California Facts

Size—3rd largest state with an area of 163,707 square miles
Population—33,871,648
State Capital—Sacramento
Statehood—September 9, 1850, the 31st state admitted to Union
State Name—Named by Spanish after *Califia,* a mythical paradise in a Spanish romance, written by Montalvo in 1510
State Elevation—*Highest:* Mt. Whitney (14,494 ft.) *Lowest:* Death Valley (282 feet below sea level)
State Song—*I Love You California,* words by F. B. Silverwood, music by A. F. Frankenstein
State Nickname—The Golden State
State Motto—*Eureka* (I have found it)
State Tree—California Redwood and the Giant Sequoia
State Marine Mammal—California Gray Whale
State Marine Fish—Garibaldi
State Mineral—Gold
State Fish—Golden Trout
State Reptile—Desert Tortoise

State Animal
Grizzly Bear

State Bird
California
Quail

State Flower
California
Poppy

Some Famous Californians

Marcus Allen, football player; **Shirley Temple Black,** actress, ambassador; **Dave Brubeck,** musician; **Julia Child,** TV chef; **Leonardo DiCaprio,** actor; **Joe DiMaggio,** baseball player; **James H. Doolittle,** general; **Isadora Duncan,** dancer; **John Fremont,** explorer; **Robert Frost,** poet; **Jerry Garcia,** guitarist, singer; **Jeff Gordon,** car racer; **William Randolph Hearst,** publisher; **Mariel Hemingway,** actress; **Sidney Howard,** playwright; **Anthony M. Kennedy,** jurist; **Jack London,** author; **George Lucas,** filmmaker; **Mark McGwire,** baseball player; **Aimee Semple McPherson,** evangelist; **Richard M. Nixon,** 37th U.S. president; **George S. Patton, Jr.,** general; **Robert Redford,** actor; **Sally K. Ride,** astronaut; **William Saroyan,** author; **Arnold Schwarzenegger,** actor/governor; **John Steinbeck,** author; **Adlai Stevenson,** statesman; **Michael Tilson Thomas,** conductor; **Earl Warren,** jurist; **Serena & Venus Williams,** tennis players; **Eldrick "Tiger" Woods,** golfer

California Division of Tourism (800) 862-2543: Website: www.state.ca.us

Creamy Shrimp Nachos

Real California Cheese—Modesto

2 cups grated QUESO BLANCO or MONTEREY JACK CHEESE
1/3 cup MAYONNAISE
4 oz. cooked SHRIMP, peeled, deveined and coarsely chopped
1/4 cup minced GREEN ONIONS
1 CHIPOTLE CHILE IN ADOBO SAUCE, puréed and strained
1 Tbsp. chopped, fresh CILANTRO LEAVES
1/2 tsp. grated LIME PEEL
1/4 tsp. ground CUMIN
SALT and PEPPER to taste
2 1/2 doz. large, flat TORTILLA CHIPS
3/4 cup grated COTIJA CHEESE
2 1/2 doz. fresh CILANTRO LEAVES

Preheat broiler. In a bowl, stir together queso blanco cheese, mayonnaise, shrimp, green onion, chipotle purée, cilantro, lime and cumin. Season with salt and pepper. Spread about 1 tablespoon of shrimp mixture onto each tortilla chip and place on a baking sheet. Broil until mixture begins to brown, about 1 minute. Sprinkle each with a generous teaspoon of cotija cheese. Add a cilantro leaf to each nacho and serve.

Chicken Chiles 'n' Cheese Popovers

Joseph Farms Cheese—Atwater

1 cup chopped cooked CHICKEN, or 1 can (5 oz.) CHICKEN, drained and flaked
1/2 cup SOUR CREAM
1 can (4 oz.) DICED GREEN CHILES, rinsed and drained
1 can (3 oz.) BLACK OLIVES, sliced and drained
1 can (8 oz.) PILLSBURY® REFRIGERATED QUICK CRESCENT DINNER ROLLS
1 cup shredded JOSEPH FARMS® MONTEREY JACK or CHEDDAR CHEESE
1 Tbsp. BUTTER or MARGARINE, melted

Preheat oven to 375°. In a bowl, combine chicken, sour cream, green chiles and olives. Separate crescent roll dough into 4 rectangles and firmly press perforations to seal. Press or roll each to form a 10 x 5 rectangle. Cut each rectangle in half crosswise, forming 8 squares. Place each square in an ungreased muffin cup, allowing dough to extend over edges. Spoon 1/4 cup chicken mixture into each cup and sprinkle with cheese. Pull four corners together; twist firmly and pinch to seal edges. Brush all with melted butter. Bake for 15-20 minutes or until golden brown. Loosen edges and remove from pan.

Los Angeles!

Known by many other names, such as "Tinsel Town" and the "City of Angels," Los Angeles has plenty to offer visitors. Visit the J. Paul Getty Center, Universal Studios Hollywood, Disneyland, La Brea Tar Pits, Griffith Observatory, Los Angeles County Museum of Art, Los Angeles Zoo, Venice Beach and Autry Museum of Western Heritage, to name just a few of the scores of interesting attractions.

Blue Cheese & Bartlett Pear Endive Bites

California Pear Advisory Board—Sacramento

8 oz. CREAM CHEESE, softened
4 oz. crumbled BLUE CHEESE
2 Tbsp. BUTTER
2 GREEN ONIONS, sliced
1/8 tsp. BLACK PEPPER
24 sm. BELGIAN ENDIVE LEAVES
1-2 ripe CALIFORNIA BARTLETT PEARS, sliced small
24 toasted WALNUT PIECES

In a food processor, combine cheeses, butter, onions and pepper; process until smooth. Transfer mixture to a pastry bag fitted with a fluted tip. Pipe into endive leaves. Add two pear slices and a piece of walnut to each.

Los Angeles is About Movie Stars!
Visit the star-studded Hollywood Walk of Fame and Grauman's Chinese Theater with its concrete impressions of more than 200 celebrity hand and footprints—including, in the case of Jimmy Durante, a nose.

Picante Guacamalsa

Serve as a dip for chips or topping for pitas and burritos.

California Avocado Commission—Santa Ana

2 CALIFORNIA AVOCADOS, **3/4 cup HOT SALSA**
peeled and chunked **1 TOMATO, chopped**
3 cloves GARLIC **1 GREEN BELL PEPPER, chopped**
1 ONION **1/2 cup GARBANZO BEANS**
2 GREEN CHILES, chopped **2 Tbsp. GOAT CHEESE (optional)**

In a blender, combine avocado, garlic, onion and chile. Process until smooth. Add salsa, tomato, bell pepper and garbanzo beans. Process a few times to combine. Pour into a bowl and top with cheese.

Southwest Spiced Walnuts

California Walnut Commission—Sacramento

2 cups CALIFORNIA WALNUT HALVES
1 Tbsp. SUGAR
1 tsp. SEA SALT
1/2 tsp. GARLIC POWDER

1/2 tsp. CUMIN
1/4 tsp. CAYENNE
1 Tbsp. WALNUT or
CANOLA OIL

Preheat oven to 375°. Spread walnuts on a baking sheet and roast about 5 minutes until golden brown. In a bowl, combine sugar, salt, garlic powder, cumin and cayenne; stir to combine. Add oil to a skillet over medium heat. Stir in toasted walnuts and seasoning; toss to coat. Cook for about 10 minutes, stirring constantly. Cool on paper towels.

The California Walnut Industry

California's first commercial walnut plantings began in 1867 when Joseph Sexton of Goleta planted English walnuts. In the late 1930s, the center of California walnut production moved to the Central Valley. California walnuts account for 99% of the commercial U.S. supply and 67% of the world's supply.

Sweet & Sour Shrimp

California Seafood Council—Sacramento

Sauce:
2 lg. unpeeled NECTARINES, chunked
3 lg. unpeeled PLUMS, chunked
3 Tbsp. APRICOT PRESERVES
5 Tbsp. DIJON MUSTARD
1/4 tsp. RED CHILE FLAKES
SALT and PEPPER to taste
Juice of 1 LEMON

1 lb. cooked SHRIMP, peeled and deveined

In a blender, combine all sauce ingredients and purée. Transfer mixture to a bowl and fold in shrimp. Cover and refrigerate until ready to serve.

Tofu Firenze

"A delicious spread for vegetables and crackers."

Billy Bramblett—Wildwood Harvest Foods, Watsonville

1 lb. WILDWOOD® FIRM TOFU
1/3 lb. fresh SPINACH, well-rinsed
1/2 cup OLIVE OIL
1/3 cup minced GARLIC
Pinch of SEA SALT

Place all ingredients in a food processor and blend on High for 4 minutes. Reduce speed to Low and slowly add the ***Herb Dressing***. Process for an additional 2 minutes. Chill well.

Herb Dressing

1/2 cup RICE VINEGAR
4 Tbsp. DIJON MUSTARD
3 Tbsp. OLIVE OIL
1/2 Tbsp. minced GARLIC
1 tsp. dried PARSLEY
1/4 tsp. OREGANO
1/2 tsp. THYME
1/4 tsp. DILL
1/4 tsp. ROSEMARY

In a food processor, combine all ingredients and blend on High for 3 minutes, scraping down sides with a rubber spatula. Pour mixture into a bowl and set aside.

La Brea Tar Pits

Rancho La Brea, known as the La Brea Tar Pits, is really a series of asphalt deposits converted into an oil byproduct that has trapped various types of plants, mammals, birds, insects and yes, even dinosaurs, since the Ice Age. Actually, what you see seeping to the surface here is asphalt, not tar!

Grilled Italian Bread with Fresh Tomatoes & Garlic

"This delicious, humble dish, which was once the mainstay of farmers and land laborers, has now been rediscovered and reinvented and can be prepared with a variety of fresh ingredients. This version is one of my favorites."

Biba Caggiano—Chef/Owner Biba Restaurant, Sacramento

1 1/2 pounds ripe, juicy TOMATOES
1-2 Tbsp. CAPERS, rinsed and patted dry
1/4 cup loosely packed, fresh OREGANO LEAVES, or 10-12 fresh
  BASIL LEAVES, shredded
SALT and freshly ground BLACK PEPPER to taste
1/3 cup EXTRA VIRGIN OLIVE OIL
8 slices crusty ITALIAN BREAD, cut 1/2-inch thick
1-2 cloves GARLIC, peeled and halved

Bring a medium-size pan of water to boil. Cut the tops off the tomatoes and carefully place them in the boiling water. Cook one or two minutes, until the skin begins to split. Cool tomatoes in a bowl of ice water. Peel, seed and roughly chop tomatoes and then place in a strainer; let drain for 20-30 minutes. In a bowl, combine tomatoes, capers and oregano and season with salt and pepper. Add olive oil and mix well. Brush bread slices lightly with more olive oil and place over a hot grill or under a broiler until golden brown on both sides. Rub hot bread slices with the garlic clove, place on serving plates and spread tomato mixture on top.

Tip: If fresh oregano or basil is unavailable, use one to two tablespoons of chopped parsley.

Stars and Movies in Los Angeles!

The Kodak Theatre is now the permanent home of the Academy Awards. When you visit Los Angeles consider taking the Warner Bros. V.I.P. Tour or going to the Universal Studios Hollywood movie theme park.

Shrimp Pacifica

Sunkist Growers, Inc.—Sherman Oaks

1 lb. med. SHRIMP, peeled, deveined and cooked
3 SUNKIST® ORANGES, peeled and cut into bite-size pieces
2 med. ONIONS, thinly sliced
3/4 cup DISTILLED WHITE or WINE VINEGAR
1/2 cup VEGETABLE OIL
1/3 cup freshly squeezed LEMON JUICE
1/4 cup KETCHUP
1 clove GARLIC, minced
2 Tbsp. SUGAR
1 Tbsp. DEHYDRATED BELL PEPPER FLAKES
1 tsp. MUSTARD SEED
1/2 tsp. CELERY SEED
1/2 tsp. SALT
1/4 tsp. PEPPER
1/4 tsp. CRUSHED RED PEPPER
2 Tbsp. chopped fresh PARSLEY
LETTUCE

In a large bowl, combine all ingredients (except parsley and lettuce); cover. Marinate in refrigerator for 8 hours or overnight, stirring occasionally.* Stir parsley into marinade. To serve, drain shrimp mixture and arrange in individual, lettuce-lined cocktail glasses or small dishes.

*Or, marinate in a tightly sealed plastic bag, turning occasionally.

Rodeo Drive Shopping District
(Ro-Day-O Drive)
Drive through the beautiful residential section in the heart of Beverly Hills until you come to this glitzy shopping district, where a well-heeled clientele shops for $200 pairs of socks wrapped in gold leaf. Window shop at Tiffany & Co., Gucci, Armani, Hermes, Harry Winston and Lladro. Visit, too, the Rodeo Collection, Cafe Rodeo and the many other famous locales along this renowned route.

Turkey-Dried Plum Lettuce Wraps

California Dried Plum Board—Sacramento

1 lb. LEAN GROUND TURKEY
2 Tbsp. finely chopped fresh GINGER
4 tsp. SOY SAUCE
2 tsp. ASIAN SESAME OIL
1 cup finely chopped DRIED PLUMS
2 Tbsp. SWEETENED COCONUT FLAKES
2 Tbsp. chopped DRY ROASTED PEANUTS
2 Tbsp. sliced GREEN ONIONS
1 Tbsp. chopped fresh CILANTRO LEAVES
8 ROMAINE LETTUCE LEAVES

In a large bowl, combine turkey, ginger, soy sauce and sesame oil; mix lightly but thoroughly. In a large nonstick skillet, brown turkey mixture over medium heat, breaking into crumbles; pour off drippings. Add dried plums, coconut, peanuts, green onion and cilantro; cook and stir 1-2 minutes or until heated through. In center of each lettuce leaf, spoon 2 tablespoonfuls turkey mixture and fold lettuce to form a small packet. Serve immediately with *Nam Pla Dipping Sauce.*

Nam Pla Dipping Sauce

1/4 cup WATER
2 Tbsp. NAM PLA (Thai fish sauce)
1 1/2 tsp. SUGAR
1 clove GARLIC, finely chopped
1/4 tsp. fresh LIME JUICE

In a small bowl, whisk together all sauce ingredients.

And of Course . . . Disneyland!

Enjoy a magical journey of breathtaking wonder, fun and adventure that only Disney could create. "The Happiest Place on Earth" is an enchanted kingdom of fantasy and imagination filled with classic family-friendly attractions, entertainment, dining and shopping.

Cheese-Spinach Appetizers

Straus Family Creamery—Marshall

2 EGGS
6 Tbsp. WHOLE-WHEAT FLOUR
1 pkg. (10 oz.) frozen SPINACH, thawed and drained
2 cups COTTAGE CHEESE
1 1/2 cups STRAUS® MEDIUM or SHARP CHEDDAR CHEESE
1/2 tsp. SEA SALT
1/4 tsp. CAYENNE PEPPER
Pinch of NUTMEG
1/4 cup BREAD CRUMBS

Preheat oven to 350° and grease a 13 x 9 baking pan. In a large bowl, beat eggs with flour until smooth. Squeeze remaining water from spinach; add spinach to egg mixture along with cottage cheese, cheddar cheese, salt, cayenne and nutmeg. Mix well. Pour mixture into prepared pan and cover with bread crumbs. Bake for about 45 minutes, until lightly browned. Cool 10 minutes and then cut into squares.

Celebrate New Year's Day!

Don't miss Pasadena's Tournament of Roses featuring the Rose Parade and the Rose Bowl Game!

Bacon Rolls

Edwards Date Shoppe—Palm Springs

1 can (8 oz.) WHOLE WATER
CHESTNUTS, drained
1 Tbsp. SOY SAUCE
1 tsp. SUGAR
1 Tbsp. DRY WHITE WINE

1 can (14 oz.) ARTICHOKE
HEARTS packed in water
1 lb. sm. MUSHROOMS
18-21 slices BACON
Fresh CHIVES (optional)

In a bowl, combine water chestnuts, soy sauce, sugar and wine and stir well. Cover and let stand for 30 minutes. Rinse artichoke hearts in cold water, drain and pat dry. Cut large artichoke hearts in halves or quarters. Preheat broiler. Cut bacon in pieces just long enough to wrap around each water chestnut, artichoke heart and mushroom; secure bacon with wooden toothpicks. Arrange in a broiler pan and broil until bacon is crisp. Serve on fresh chives, if desired.

Tomato, Avocado & Goat Cheese Crostini

This is a quick and elegant cocktail snack.

California Tomato Commission—Fresno

1 FRENCH BAGUETTE
1/3 cup OLIVE OIL
2 tsp. fresh minced GARLIC
2 ripe AVOCADOS, diced
4 oz. MILD GOAT CHEESE (Chèvre recommended)
3/4 tsp. SALT
1 1/2 cups seeded, diced CALIFORNIA ROMA TOMATOES
2 Tbsp. EXTRA VIRGIN OLIVE OIL
1/4 tsp. PEPPER
1/4 cup chopped fresh BASIL
Small BASIL LEAVES for garnish (optional)

Preheat oven to 350°. Slice bread into 1/4-inch thick diagonal slices. In a small bowl, blend together olive oil and garlic. Brush bread lightly with garlic oil and arrange on baking sheets in a single layer. Bake for 10-15 minutes or until golden brown and crisp; remove from oven and let cool. In a bowl, combine avocado, goat cheese and 1/2 of the salt, mixing until smooth. In a separate bowl, combine tomato, olive oil, remaining salt, pepper and basil. Spread each toasted slice with 1 tablespoon of avocado mixture and top with tomato-basil mixture. Garnish with basil leaves, if desired.

Note: If making avocado mixture in advance, bury avocado pit in the mixture to prevent browning. Crostini can be made ahead of time and stored in an airtight container. Let cool completely before storing.

Makes 35-40 pieces.

Knott's Berry Farm

Knott's Berry Farm, the nation's oldest and first theme park, draws around five million visitors each year. It has 165 rides, shows, attractions and restaurants as well as special events for the Holidays. Try the "Perilous Plunge," the world's highest and steepest water ride!

Artichoke Heart Omelets

Monica Fuchs and Beverley Bennett—The Philo Pottery Inn, Philo

TOMATO SALSA
2 cans (10 oz. ea.) ARTICHOKE HEARTS, packed in water
1 cup shredded PARMESAN CHEESE
2 cups shredded SHARP CHEDDAR CHEESE
12 EGGS
1 pint SOUR CREAM

Preheat oven to 375°. Grease a 13 x 9 baking dish. Spread a thin layer of salsa on the bottom of dish. Drain and chop artichoke hearts and spread over salsa. Layer Parmesan cheese over artichokes and sprinkle cheddar cheese on top. In a blender, combine eggs and sour cream and blend well. Pour egg mixture over cheese. Bake for 35-40 minutes or until eggs are set and center is solid. Garnish with **snipped fresh CHIVES**.

Norma Jean, Artichoke Queen?

Castroville is known as the Artichoke Capital of the World. In 1948 a young woman named Norma Jean was crowned Castroville's first Artichoke Queen. She went on to become actress Marilyn Monroe.

Egg & Chorizo Enchiladas

MexGrocer.com (Recipe courtesy of Mission Foods)—La Jolla

Enchiladas:
1 clove GARLIC
2 Tbsp. chopped ONION
3 SERRANO CHILES, diced
4 oz. CHORIZO, crumbled
3 EGGS, beaten
2 tsp. chopped CILANTRO
SALT to taste

12 MISSION® FLOUR TORTILLAS

Salsa:
2 Tbsp. Oil
2 cloves GARLIC
2 Tbsp. diced ONION
2 ANCHO CHILES, chopped
4 CHIPOTLE CHILES, chopped
2 ARBOL CHILES, chopped
8 TOMATILLOS
1/2 cup ORANGE JUICE
1/2 cup CHICKEN STOCK
SALT and PEPPER to taste

Garnish:
3/4 cup shredded PANELA CHEESE
1/4 ONION, chopped
1 AVOCADO, sliced
1/4 cup CREAM

In a skillet, sauté garlic, onion, serrano chiles and chorizo until onions are translucent. Add eggs, cilantro and salt. Cook until eggs are done. Divide egg mixture between the tortillas; roll up and place on serving dishes. To make salsa: In a skillet, add oil and sauté garlic, onion, chiles and tomatilloes; add the orange juice and chicken stock and boil until mixture has thickened. Mash mixture in pan. Season with salt and pepper and pour over enchiladas. To garnish, sprinkle with panela cheese and onions and top with avocado slices and cream.

Mushroom Strata

Peirano Estate Vineyards—Acampo

1/4 lb. PANCETTA (Italian bacon)	1 1/4 cups MILK
5 GREEN ONIONS, sliced	1 loaf of day-old FRENCH
1 1/2 lbs. MUSHROOMS, sliced	BREAD
SALT and PEPPER to taste	1 cup grated SWISS CHEESE
1/3 cup PEIRANO ESTATE	5 EGGS, beaten
VINEYARDS® CHARDONNAY	1/2 cup HEAVY CREAM

Preheat oven to 350°. Slice pancetta into 1/4-inch pieces; sauté over medium/low heat for 10 minutes. Add green onions and sauté briefly. Add mushrooms and sauté until cooked; remove from heat and season with salt and pepper. In a shallow dish, mix the wine and milk. Slice bread into 1/2-inch pieces and dip into wine mixture. Place bread in a buttered 12-inch round or oval gratin dish; cover with mushroom mixture and sprinkle with cheese. Cover with another layer of bread dipped in milk. Season beaten eggs with salt and pepper and pour evenly over layers. Cover and refrigerate overnight. Remove strata from refrigerator and allow to reach room temperature. Drizzle with cream and bake for 45 minutes or until puffy and browned.

Places to Visit in San Diego

San Diego's Gaslamp Quarter offers dining, shopping and entertainment in an historic setting. Qualcomm Stadium accommodates a variety of events, including sports and concerts. Balboa Park is home to fifteen museums, various arts and international culture associations, as well as the world-famous San Diego Zoo, making it one of the nation's largest and most popular cultural and entertainment complexes. A visit to the San Diego Wild Animal Park is like a safari to many of the world's most exotic places. SeaWorld San Diego has hosted more than 100 million guests since opening in 1964. The San Diego Padres major league baseball team now plays in the new Petco Park.

Artichoke & Swiss Cheese Soufflés

"Whether you use fresh or canned artichokes, this is a great breakfast treat."

Kristina Tellefsen—Santa Nella House Bed & Breakfast, Guerneville

1 can (14 oz.) ARTICHOKE HEARTS packed in water
4 lg. EGGS, separated
1/4 cup BUTTER
1/4 cup FLOUR
1 1/2 cups MILK
1/2 tsp. SALT
1 tsp. WORCESTERSHIRE SAUCE
1/8 tsp. CAYENNE
1/8 tsp. WHITE PEPPER
1/2 lb. SWISS CHEESE, grated

Preheat oven to 375°. Drain artichokes well and chop coarsely; set aside. Beat egg whites until stiff peaks form; set aside. In a saucepan, melt butter over low heat. Add flour and stir with a wire whisk until blended. In a separate saucepan, bring milk to a boil. Pour milk into flour mixture and whisk vigorously until smooth and thickened (the thicker the final mixture, the better the soufflés rise). Season with salt, Worcestershire sauce, cayenne and white pepper. Remove from heat. Add Swiss cheese and stir until melted. Beat in egg yolks. Add artichokes to the cheese mixture and fold in egg whites. Pour mixture into 6 ungreased, individual heatproof soufflé dishes; place in a roasting pan filled with 1/2 inch of hot water. Bake on top shelf for 30 minutes or until set. Serve immediately.

Anza-Borrego Desert State Park

With over 600,000 acres, Anza-Borrego Desert State Park® in the Colorado Desert, is the largest desert state park in the contiguous United States. It includes 500 miles of dirt roads, two huge wilderness areas and 110 miles of riding and hiking trails.

Blueberry Stuffed French Toast

"My Irish grandmother made this for special occasion brunches."

Kim Thomas—Inn of Imagination, Napa

12 slices day-old WHITE BREAD, crusts removed, cut into 1-inch cubes
2 pkgs. (8 oz. ea.) CREAM CHEESE, cut into 1-inch cubes
1 cup fresh or frozen BLUEBERRIES
12 EGGS
2 cups MILK
1/3 cup MAPLE SYRUP or HONEY

In a greased 13 x 9 baking dish, layer half of the bread and cover with cream cheese. Top with blueberries and cover with remaining bread. In a bowl, beat eggs; add milk and syrup and mix well. Pour egg mixture over bread. Cover and chill for at least 8 hours. Remove from refrigerator 30 minutes before baking. Bake, covered, at 350° for 30 minutes. Uncover and bake an additional 25-30 minutes or until the top is golden brown and center is set. Serve with *Blueberry Sauce.*

Blueberry Sauce

1 cup SUGAR
2 Tbsp. CORNSTARCH
1 cup WATER
1 cup fresh or frozen BLUEBERRIES
1 Tbsp. BUTTER

In a saucepan, combine sugar and cornstarch. Add water and bring to a boil. Boil for 3 minutes over medium heat, stirring constantly. Stir in blueberries. Reduce heat and simmer 8-10 minutes or until berries have burst. Stir in butter until melted.

Coronado Island and "The Del"

Considered to be one of the most beautiful resorts in America, The Hotel del Coronado, is a classic historic hotel. It was built in 1888 and designated a National Historic Landmark in 1977.

Salsa Jack Soufflé

"This soufflé is one of the many Hispanic-style recipes served at our Inn. A large Hispanic population settled in Murphys during the Gold Rush era."

Barbara Costa—Dunbar House, 1880, Murphys

5 CORN TORTILLAS, torn into bite-size pieces
10 Tbsp. SALSA
10 EGGS
1/2 cup FLOUR
1/2 tsp. SALT
2 cups SMALL CURD COTTAGE CHEESE
2 cups grated MONTEREY JACK CHEESE
2 cups grated CHEDDAR CHEESE
4 oz. diced, seeded GREEN CHILES (hot or mild)
1/4 cup chopped RED PIMENTO
1 can (15 oz.) CORN, drained
2 dashes TABASCO®

Topping:
    SUN-DRIED TOMATOES IN OIL, julienned
    FRENCH FRIED ONIONS

SALSA

Spray 10 ramekins with cooking spray and line with tortilla pieces. Top with 1 tablespoon of salsa. In a bowl, beat eggs until light and add remaining ingredients; mix well. Divide egg mixture evenly between dishes. Bake at 350° for 30 minutes. Remove from oven; top with sun-dried tomatoes and sprinkle with french fried onions. Return to oven and continue to bake for 5 minutes. Serve immediately with salsa on the side.

The Navy in San Diego

Naval Air Station North Island is part of the largest aerospace-industrial complex in the Navy, the 57,000-acre Naval Base Coronado. NASNI, with only its commands in the metropolitan San Diego Area, brackets the city of Coronado from the entrance of San Diego Bay to the Mexican border.

Souflatta

*"Excellent when served with German potato pancakes
and a good breakfast sausage."*

Paula Stanbridge—Windrose Inn, Jackson

1 tsp. CANOLA OIL or COOKING SPRAY
10 lg. EGGS
1/4 cup + 2 Tbsp. ALL PURPOSE FLOUR
1 tsp. BAKING POWDER
1/2 tsp. SALT
2 cups shredded SHARP CHEDDAR CHEESE, 2 Tbsp. reserved
1 cup shredded fresh PARMIGIANO-REGGIANO
    CHEESE, 2 Tbsp. reserved
8 oz. RICOTTA CHEESE
1 cup finely chopped GREEN ONIONS, 2 Tbsp. reserved
1/2 cup finely chopped RED BELL PEPPER
8 thin slices RED BELL PEPPER
PARSLEY (optional)
4 Tbsp. SOUR CREAM

Preheat oven to 350°. Grease a 9-inch glass or ceramic pie
pan with canola oil and set aside. In a mixer, beat eggs on
medium-high for 8-10 minutes, until light and fluffy (doubled in
volume). In a bowl, sift together flour, baking powder and salt;
add to eggs and mix on medium-high for 2 minutes. Add
cheddar, Parmesan and ricotta cheeses, green onions and
chopped bell pepper and mix on low speed for 2 minutes. Pour
mixture into pie pan and bake for 55 minutes. Remove from
oven and let stand for 5 minutes. Slice and arrange each wedge
on a plate. Sprinkle with reserved cheddar and Parmesan
cheese and top with green onions. Place a slice of bell pepper on
top of each wedge and sprinkle with parsley. Add a dollop of sour
cream and serve immediately.

Old Point Loma Lighthouse

*The Old Point Loma Lighthouse stood watch
over the entrance to San Diego Bay for 36 years
(1855-1891). Today it still stands as a sentinel
to a vanished past.*

Wade, JW

Marinated Artichoke Strata

"This is a favorite among our guests."

Debra La Rochelle—Sutter Creek Inn, Sutter Creek

12 EGGS
2 cups MILK
2 tsp. TARRAGON
1/4 tsp. GARLIC SALT
1/4 tsp. ONION POWDER
1/4 tsp. PEPPER
10 slices SOURDOUGH BREAD, torn into pieces
1/2 cup shredded SWISS CHEESE
1/2 cup shredded MONTEREY JACK CHEESE
1 cup diced fresh MUSHROOMS
1 cup MARINATED ARTICHOKE HEARTS, drained and chopped

Preheat oven to 350°. In a bowl, beat together eggs and milk. Add tarragon, garlic salt, onion powder and pepper. Place bread on the bottom of a greased 13 x 9 baking dish. Pour egg mixture over bread. Top with remaining ingredients. Let bread soak for 30 minutes. Bake for 45-60 minutes or until puffy and golden.

Stuffed French Toast

J. Patrick House Bed & Breakfast Inn—Cambria

1 1/2 loaves SHEEPHERDER'S
    BREAD
10 EGGS
3 cups MILK
3/4 cup PURE MAPLE SYRUP

1 pkg. (16 oz.) CREAM
    CHEESE, cubed
1 BANANA, mashed
Pinch of SALT

Butter a 13 x 9 baking dish. Cut bread into 1-inch cubes and place in a bowl. In another bowl, beat together remaining ingredients. Pour egg mixture over bread and mix well with a rubber spatula. Transfer mixture to baking dish and press down to flatten. Cover and refrigerate overnight. In the morning, remove from refrigerator and let sit for 20 minutes at room temperature. Bake at 350° for 40-50 minutes or until golden brown.

Kiwifruit
Sweet Omelet

California Kiwifruit Commission—El Dorado Hills

3-4 CALIFORNIA KIWIFRUIT, pared and sliced
6 Tbsp. POWDERED SUGAR
2 Dashes of CINNAMON
4 EGGS, separated
1/8 tsp. SALT
1/2 tsp. grated LEMON PEEL
2 Tbsp. BUTTER or MARGARINE

Place kiwifruit in a shallow dish and sprinkle with 2 tablespoons powdered sugar and a dash of cinnamon. Let stand 20 minutes; turn occasionally. Beat egg whites and salt until soft peaks form. Gradually add 2 tablespoons powdered sugar; beat until stiff. Beat egg yolks until thick; add lemon peel. Fold into whites. Heat butter in 10-inch ovenproof skillet. Stir in 1 tablespoon powdered sugar and a dash cinnamon. Pour in egg mixture; smooth surface. Cook over medium heat 3-5 minutes or until eggs are puffed and set and bottom is golden brown. Bake at 325° for 10 minutes or until knife inserted near center comes out clean. Loosen edge of omelet. Make a shallow cut, slightly off center, through top. Arrange kiwifruit over larger section. Fold smaller portion over kiwifruit. Serve on a warm platter sprinkled with additional powdered sugar.

Outdoor San Diego

Mission Bay Park, the West Coast's largest man-made aquatic park, covers more than 4,000 acres and offers a wide range of recreational activities. Mission Trails Regional Park encompasses nearly 5,800 acres of both natural and developed recreational areas for hiking and overnight camping.

Guido's Sourdough Pancakes

"We inherited the sourdough starter we use today from my husband's grandfather, Guido Galucci. It is thought to be well over 100 years old. The culture lives, jarred, in our refrigerator. As we use it, we replenish it by adding flour and milk to the jar. We use our starter to make sourdough French bread San Francisco style, pancakes, waffles and more."

Debra Winters—Forest Manor Bed & Breakfast, Angwin

1 cup EVAPORATED MILK	2 Tbsp. SUGAR
1 cup WARM WATER	1/2 tsp. SALT
1 3/4-2 cups unsifted FLOUR	1 1/2 tsp. BAKING SODA
2 EGGS	OIL or BUTTER

The night before, combine 1/2 cup **Sourdough Starter,** evaporated milk, water and flour in a large bowl; mix to blend and leave at room temperature overnight. The next morning, add eggs, sugar, salt and baking soda and mix well *(do not beat)*. Cook pancakes over moderate heat on a griddle greased with oil or butter. Turn when top side is full of broken bubbles and has lost its glossiness. Serve topped with fresh fruit and hot maple or blueberry syrup.

Makes 12 six-inch pancakes.

Sourdough Starter

(Note: this is <u>not</u> the Galucci secret sourdough recipe.)

2 cups WARM WATER	2 cups FLOUR
1 pkg. active DRY YEAST	1/4 tsp. SUGAR

In a glass or ceramic bowl, pour 1/2 cup of warm water. Add yeast and let dissolve. Add flour, sugar and remaining water to mixture. Mix well; cover with a towel and set in a warm place for at least 48 hours. Refrigerate, loosely covered.

Soups & Salads

Avocado Soup

California Avocado Commission—Santa Ana

8 Tbsp. BUTTER
8 Tbsp. FLOUR
6 cups MILK
4 ripe AVOCADOS, peeled
   and mashed
1 1/2 Tbsp. LIME JUICE

1/4 tsp. GARLIC POWDER
1 Tbsp. SANGRÍA
SOUR CREAM
Thin slices of LIME
BASIL

In a saucepan, melt butter and stir in flour. Add 4 cups milk slowly and blend well; set aside to cool. In a blender, mix avocados with lime juice, adding 2 cups of milk and garlic powder. Whisk avocado mixture into the cooled milk mixture. Blend in wine. Chill and serve cold, garnished with sour cream, lime slices and basil.

Avocado Capital of the World!

Fallbrook, in San Diego County, is known as the avocado capital of the world! Avocados were first planted in Fallbrook in 1912 and they have flourished ever since.

Apple & California Cheddar Cheese Soup

Real California Cheese—Modesto

2 Tbsp. UNSALTED BUTTER
4 cups peeled and chopped GRANNY SMITH APPLES
1 cup peeled and diced RUSSET POTATOES
1/3 cup diced CELERY
1/2 cup diced ONION
1/4 tsp. THYME
1/4 cup WHITE WINE
4 cups CHICKEN STOCK
3 cups shredded WHITE CHEDDAR CHEESE
SALT and PEPPER to taste
NUTMEG to taste
1/4 cup HEAVY CREAM

Melt butter in a large saucepan over medium heat. Sauté apples, potatoes, celery, onion and thyme until onions are translucent, about 10 minutes. Add white wine to deglaze the pan. Cook about 1 minute. Add chicken stock, bring to a boil, reduce heat and simmer for 30 minutes. Transfer to a blender and purée until smooth. Over medium heat, reheat soup and slowly add cheese, seasonings and cream. Cook until cheese is melted and soup is hot, but *do not boil*. Garnish as desired.

Hearst Castle

Built on a mountain overlooking the city of San Simeon and the Pacific Ocean, Hearst Castle was once the home of William Randolph Hearst, a wealthy newspaper publisher. The main residence, Casa Grande, has displays of Hearst's art collection and antiques. This 165-room, 127-acre estate includes pools, fountains and statuary that grace the landscaped gardens.

Puerco Loco Stew

Anne Air—Everett Ridge Vineyards & Winery, Healdsburg

2 Tbsp. CHILI POWDER
1 tsp. SALT
1 tsp. ground BLACK PEPPER
2 1/2 lbs. boneless PORK, cut into 2-inch pieces
3 slices BACON, chopped
1 lg. ONION, thinly sliced
1 cup diced SMOKED HAM
1 med. CARROT, peeled and chopped
6 cloves GARLIC, chopped
2 POBLANO CHILES, seeded and cut into 2-inch x 1/4-inch strips
2 cups drained HOMINY
1 cup diced TOMATOES, drained
1 1/2 cups EVERETT RIDGE® ZINFANDEL
1 cup CHICKEN BROTH
1 tsp. MARJORAM
1/4 cup chopped fresh CILANTRO

In a bowl, combine one tablespoon chili powder, salt and pepper. Rub mixture over pork; set aside. In a large heavy pot over medium heat, cook bacon until crisp; remove and drain on paper towels. Working in batches, brown the pork in bacon drippings, about ten minutes per batch. As pork is browned, use a slotted spoon to transfer to a bowl. When all pork has cooked, reduce heat to medium. Add onion, ham, carrot and garlic to pot; cover and cook five minutes, stirring occasionally to scrape up browned bits. Add chiles; stir one minute. Stir in hominy, tomatoes, wine, broth, marjoram, pork and remaining chili powder and bring to a boil. Reduce heat; cover and simmer until pork is tender, about one hour. Simmer stew uncovered until slightly reduced and thickened, about ten minutes. Season to taste with additional salt and pepper. Spoon into serving bowls and garnish with cilantro.

Suggested wine: Everett Ridge® Zinfandel.

Hollywood!

In Los Angeles, high atop Mt. Lee, is the world-renowned Hollywood sign. It is 450 feet long with letters 45 feet high!

Chilled Cucumber & Avocado Soup

Ironstone's Executive Chef, Daniel Lewis, lives by the philosophy, "Eat well, drink wine and live large." An expert in wine and food pairing, he believes that in many ways "fusion" cuisine started way back during the Gold Rush—a natural result of the cultural and culinary blend created by the arrival of fortune seekers from all over the world. Dan often draws his inspiration from the colorful characters and menus of yesteryear, as well as the bounty provided by his surroundings at Ironstone—from miner's lettuce plucked from a nearby stream, to figs from the 100-year-old tree that adorns the Ironstone main lawn.

Executive Chef Dan Lewis—Ironstone Winery, Murphys

4 AVOCADOS, peeled and seeded
2 tsp. LEMON JUICE
1 ENGLISH CUCUMBER, peeled and chopped
1 bunch CHIVES, chopped
4 cups CHICKEN STOCK
2 cups CREAM
1/2 cup SOUR CREAM
SALT and PEPPER to taste

Purée avocados and lemon juice in a food processor. Add cucumber and half of the chives and purée until smooth. Add chicken stock, cream and sour cream; adjust salt and pepper to taste. Garnish with remaining chives.

Suggested wine: Ironstone Vineyards® Viognier

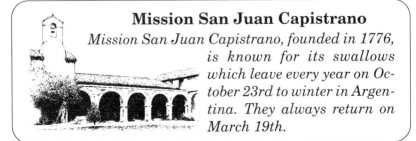

Mission San Juan Capistrano

Mission San Juan Capistrano, founded in 1776, is known for its swallows which leave every year on October 23rd to winter in Argentina. They always return on March 19th.

California Cioppino

California Seafood Council—Sacramento

1/4 cup OLIVE OIL
3 cloves GARLIC, minced
1 ONION, chopped
1/2 cup chopped CELERY TOPS
1/4 tsp. CRUSHED RED PEPPER
1/2 cup chopped fresh PARSLEY
2 cups WINE or CHICKEN STOCK
2 cups chopped TOMATOES
1 BAY LEAF
1 tsp. chopped fresh OREGANO
1 tsp. chopped fresh BASIL
2-3 lbs. assorted SEAFOOD*
PARSLEY
LEMON WEDGES

In a large, heavy stockpot, heat oil and sauté garlic, onion, celery tops, crushed red pepper and parsley until onion is translucent. Add wine, tomatoes, bay leaf, oregano and basil. Bring to a boil. Lower heat, cover and simmer for 20 minutes. Add seafood, beginning with varieties needing longer cooking time, and simmer for approximately 20 more minutes. Remove from heat and ladle into soup bowls. Garnish with parsley and lemon wedges. Serve with garlic bread on the side.

*Assortment may include California shrimp, crab, spiny lobster, clams, mussels, rockfish or halibut.

Pomegranate Salad

"My mother developed this colorful, delicious salad."

Bonnie Brown—China Ranch Date Farm & Bakery, Tecopa

6 med. POMEGRANATES, halved
1 lg. RED BELL PEPPER, diced
5 GREEN ONIONS, chopped
1/4 cup chopped fresh CILANTRO
1 can (20 oz.) PINEAPPLE TIDBITS, with juice

Gently scoop out pomegranate seeds into a bowl. Add remaining ingredients and mix well.

Warm Salmon Soba Salad with Currant Dressing

A dressy dish with lots of style, bursting with color, texture and opposing elements. It's sweet and sour, warm and cold, soft and crunchy, and bejeweled with tiny currants.

California Raisins Marketing Board—Fresno

8 oz. SOBA NOODLES
2 Tbsp. VEGETABLE OIL
4 (6 oz. ea.) skinless SALMON FILLETS
KOSHER SALT to taste
Freshly ground BLACK PEPPER to taste
8 cups MIXED SALAD GREENS
1 cup thinly sliced ENGLISH CUCUMBER
2 med. GREEN ONIONS, sliced diagonally
1 (4 oz.) piece DAIKON RADISH, julienned
2 lg. ORANGES, segmented

Bring 8 cups of lightly salted water to a boil and cook the noodles for 3-4 minutes or until just tender *(do not overcook)*. Cool noodles under cold running water; toss with 1 tablespoon vegetable oil and refrigerate, tightly covered, until needed. Season the salmon with salt and pepper. Heat the remaining oil in a large sauté pan over medium-high heat. Sauté salmon fillets for 2-3 minutes on each side (or to desired doneness). Keep warm. Arrange a base of the greens on each of 4 salad plates. In a mixing bowl, toss the noodles, cucumber, green onion, daikon and orange segments with half of the ***Currant Dressing.*** Place a mound of the dressed noodle mixture in the center of the greens. Top each salad with a warm salmon fillet and drizzle the remaining dressing over all.

(See *Currant Dressing* recipe on next page)

The Hollywood Bowl

The Hollywood Bowl is the world's largest natural amphi-theater, seating over 17,000 for a wide variety of events. Drop in to take a free look at the famous white shell or even attend free rehearsals during the summer hours!

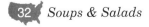

Warm Salmon Soba Salad with Currant Dressing
(continued from previous page)

Currant Dressing

Can be prepared two days ahead. Cover tightly and refrigerate.

2 tsp. WASABI PASTE or 2 Tbsp. DIJON MUSTARD
4 Tbsp. EXTRA VIRGIN OLIVE OIL
1/4 cup JAPANESE SEASONED RICE VINEGAR
JUICE of 1 LEMON
1/4 cup frozen ORANGE JUICE CONCENTRATE, thawed
2 Tbsp. PICKLED GINGER, minced
1/2 cup CALIFORNIA ZANTE CURRANTS
SALT and freshly ground PEPPER

Combine dressing ingredients in a small bowl; whisk together. Set aside.

Big Bear Lake

Nestled in the San Bernardino Mountains, this area provides abundant recreational opportunities. Two of Southern California's largest ski resorts, Snow Summit Mountain Resort and Bear Mountain Resort, can be found here.

Asian Coleslaw

Mariquita Farms—Watsonville

1/2 head CABBAGE, shredded
2-3 CARROTS, grated
2 tsp. KOSHER or SEA SALT
1 ONION, chopped
1 Tbsp. TOASTED SESAME OIL
4 Tbsp. RICE VINEGAR
4 Tbsp. SALAD OIL

1 tsp. SOY SAUCE
1 Tbsp. MIRIN (optional)
1 Tbsp. chopped fresh CILANTRO
1/3 cup + 1 Tbsp. toasted SESAME SEEDS

In a colander placed over a bowl, toss cabbage and carrots with salt. Let stand for 3-4 hours, until cabbage wilts. Rinse cabbage mixture; drain and dry with towels. In a glass salad bowl, toss cabbage mixture with remaining ingredients (except 1 tablespoon sesame seeds). Cover and refrigerate at least an hour. When serving, sprinkle with reserved sesame seeds.

California
Fig & Citrus Salad

California Fresh Fig Growers Association—Fresno

Dressing:
- 1/3 cup ORANGE JUICE
- 2 Tbsp. BALSAMIC VINEGAR
- 2 Tbsp. OLIVE OIL
- 1 Tbsp. HONEY
- 1/4 tsp. SALT
- 1/8 tsp. CRUSHED RED PEPPER

2 **NAVEL ORANGES,** peeled and sliced crosswise
8 lg. fresh **CALIFORNIA BLACK or GREEN FIGS,**
    sliced lengthwise 1/4-inch thick
1 **RED ONION,** thinly sliced
1 bunch **SPINACH LEAVES**
1/3 cup broken **WALNUTS,** toasted*

In a blender, combine all dressing ingredients and blend until thoroughly mixed. Place fruit and onion in a large mixing bowl. Pour dressing over all. Set aside for 10 minutes to an hour. To serve, line individual salad plates with spinach leaves. Spoon dressing mixture and fruit on top and sprinkle each with about 1 tablespoon of walnuts.

*Spread walnuts in a shallow ungreased baking pan. Bake at 300° for 5-7 minutes or until lightly browned, stirring once or twice.

Joshua Tree National Park

Located near Twentynine Palms, this 800,000-acre park was set aside to protect the unique assembly of natural resources brought together by the junction of two of California's ecosystems: the Colorado Desert (occupying the eastern portion) and the Mohave Desert (with its Joshua tree forests) in the west.

Smoked Salmon Salad

Stella Cadente Olive Oil Co./Boonville General Store—Boonville

1 lb. PENNE or FUSILLI PASTA
6 oz. SMOKED SALMON
1 Tbsp. fresh LEMON JUICE
3 Tbsp. STELLA CADENTE™ MEYER LEMON OIL
SALT and freshly ground BLACK PEPPER to taste
Grated PEEL of 1 LEMON
2 Tbsp. chopped fresh GARLIC CHIVES
2 Tbsp. chopped fresh ITALIAN PARSLEY
2 Tbsp. rinsed and minced CAPERS
MIXED GREENS

Boil pasta in salted water until *al dente* and rinse under cold water. Shred salmon into pieces just smaller than the pasta. In a small bowl, whisk together the lemon juice, lemon oil, salt and pepper. In a large bowl, toss together the pasta, salmon, lemon peel, chives, parsley and capers. Drizzle the dressing over the pasta mixture and toss lightly to coat. Serve on a bed of mixed greens.

California Albacore Salad

California Seafood Council—Sacramento

1 lb. CALIFORNIA ALBACORE*, poached
2 cans (15 oz. ea.) WHITE BEANS, drained
1/2 cup minced RED ONION
1/2 cup chopped GOLDEN BELL PEPPER
1/2 cup chopped fresh PARSLEY
1/2 cup oil-packed SUN-DRIED TOMATOES, chopped
2 cloves GARLIC, minced
1/2 tsp. BLACK PEPPER
1/2 tsp. dried BASIL or 1 Tbsp. chopped fresh BASIL
4 Tbsp. LEMON JUICE
2 Tbsp. EXTRA VIRGIN OLIVE OIL

In a large bowl, break albacore into bite-size pieces. Add remaining ingredients and gently toss. Cover and refrigerate at least 4 hours before serving.

*May substitute Spanish mackerel or bonito for albacore.

Grilled Salmon & Bartlett Pear Salad

California Pear Advisory Board—Sacramento

4 (6 oz. ea.) SALMON FILLETS
4 cups BABY GREENS
2 ripe CALIFORNIA BARTLETT PEARS, cored and thinly sliced
1/3 cup chopped, toasted HAZELNUTS

Gently rinse salmon fillets and pat dry. Drizzle each fillet with 1/2 tablespoon *Lemon Vinaigrette*. Place salmon on a lightly oiled grill over medium coals for 8 to 12 minutes or until salmon just begins to flake easily, turning once halfway through grilling time. Toss the greens with half of the vinaigrette and assemble on a large platter. Top greens with pears, hazelnuts and salmon fillets. Drizzle with remaining vinaigrette.

Lemon Vinaigrette

3/4 cup OLIVE OIL
1/4 cup BALSAMIC VINEGAR
2 Tbsp. LEMON JUICE
2 Tbsp. HONEY
1 tsp. SALT
1/2 tsp. freshly ground PEPPER

In a bowl, whisk together all ingredients.

Chimol

*This Salvadoran salsa recipe is a traditional topping for beef,
fish or chicken. It's also great on scrambled eggs!*

Mariquita Farms—Watsonville

2 ICICLE RADISHES, finely chopped
3 TOMATOES, finely chopped
1 ONION, finely chopped
1 bunch fresh CILANTRO, finely chopped
2-3 pinches of SALT
JUICE of 1 LEMON

In a bowl, combine all the ingredients and mix well. Let sit for at least 30 minutes for flavors to blend.

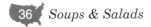

Ravishing Radicchio Salad

"My hope is to be able to assist all California schools in the development of their own gardens."

Chef Andy Powning—GreenLeaf Produce, San Francisco

2 med. BEETS
1 clove GARLIC
1 head BUTTER LETTUCE, torn into 3-inch pieces
1 sm. head RADICCHIO, thinly sliced
Toasted PECANS to taste
1 COMICE PEAR, peeled, halved and thinly sliced
2-4 oz. GORGONZOLA CHEESE, crumbled

Roast beets in a 350° oven for 45 minutes or until fork tender; cool, peel and slice. Rub a large wooden salad bowl with garlic. Add lettuce, radicchio, beets, pecans and pear slices. Add *Pistachio Vinaigrette* to salad and toss. Top with Gorgonzola.

Pistachio Vinaigrette

1/4 cup PISTACHIO OIL
3 Tbsp. BALSAMIC VINEGAR (or to taste)
JUICE of 1/2 LEMON
SALT and PEPPER to taste
DIJON MUSTARD to taste

In small bowl, combine all ingredients and mix well.

Catalina Island

The Santa Catalina Island Conservancy, a non-profit operating foundation, now owns about 88% of this island's 76 square miles. Avalon, a city occupying just over 1 square  *mile, has a population of about 3,200—although summer and weekend population counts rise to over 10,000. Travel to Catalina by air or sea (it's just 22 miles off California's coast) and enjoy hiking, golf, fishing, boating and many other relaxing and recreational activities.*

Orzo & Lentil Salad

"This is a favorite dish that we serve at our Inn."

Cyrus Griffin, Chef/Owner—Sonoma Coast Villa Inn & Spa,
Bodega

1 cup PETITE FRENCH GREEN
   LENTILS (organic)
2 cups ORZO PASTA
2 qts. WATER
1/4 cup OIL
2 Tbsp. CURRY POWDER
1 Tbsp. GRANULATED GARLIC
1 Tbsp. CUMIN

2 Tbsp. SOY SAUCE
1/4 cup RED WINE VINEGAR
1-2 cups VEGETABLES* (cut
   to size of pasta)
Grated PEEL of 1 ORANGE
JUICE of 2 LEMONS
SALT and PEPPER to taste

Wash and cull lentils and then place in a saucepan and cover with two inches of water. Bring to a boil and simmer, covered, for 20-25 minutes or until tender yet firm. Drain excess water and chill. Cook orzo in boiling, salted water for about 10 minutes and drain. Add oil and combine until all pasta is coated. Combine orzo with lentils in a large mixing bowl. Add spices and remaining ingredients. Mix all together and chill.

* If including vegetables such as carrots, celery, corn or bell pepper, blanch before chopping and adding to orzo mix. Zucchini and yellow squash need not be blanched.

Greek Shrimp Salad

Contessa Food Products—San Pedro

12 oz. colossal 21/25 CONTESSA® COOKED TAIL-OFF SHRIMP,
   thawed
10-12 TOMATOES, each cut into 8 wedges
3 CUCUMBERS, cut into 1/4-inch rounds
1 cup FETA CHEESE, crumbled
8 oz. GREEK SALAD DRESSING
SALT and PEPPER to taste
1 can (6 oz.) WHOLE OLIVES (optional)

In a large bowl, add all ingredients and mix well. Cover and refrigerate for at least 1 hour before serving.

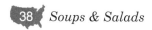

Poached Salmon Salad with Raspberry-Orange Vinaigrette

California King Salmon Council—Folsom

4 (6 oz. ea.) fresh CALIFORNIA KING SALMON® FILLETS
2 cups WHITE WINE or VEGETABLE BROTH
2 cups CLAM JUICE or FISH STOCK
1 LEMON, quartered
2 MINT SPRIGS
8 oz. MIXED SALAD GREENS
2 cups fresh PINEAPPLE, cubed and well-drained
1 1/3 cups fresh RASPBERRIES
2 KIWIFRUIT, peeled and sliced
Chopped fresh CILANTRO to taste

Rinse salmon fillets and set aside. In a medium skillet or fish poacher, bring wine, clam juice, lemon and mint sprigs to a boil. Add salmon, skin-side up. Reduce heat to a simmer and cook, covered, for 8-10 minutes or until salmon is cooked through. Remove salmon from poaching liquid; cool to room temperature and remove skin. Arrange salad greens on four large dinner plates. Place a salmon fillet on top of greens and surround with pineapple, raspberries and kiwifruit. Drizzle with *Raspberry-Orange Vinaigrette* and sprinkle with cilantro.

Raspberry-Orange Vinaigrette

1/2 cup RASPBERRY VINEGAR
1/4 cup ORANGE JUICE
3 Tbsp. OLIVE OIL
3 Tbsp. chopped MINT LEAVES

3 Tbsp. minced SHALLOTS
1 Tbsp. HONEY
1/2 tsp. SALT
1/8 tsp. WHITE PEPPER

In a small bowl, whisk together all ingredients.

Did You Know?
The first motion picture theater opened in Los Angeles on April 2, 1902.

Bing Cherry & Smoked Turkey Romaine Salad

California Cherry Advisory Board—Lodi

1 head ROMAINE LETTUCE, chopped
1/2 cup crumbled FETA CHEESE
1/4 cup diced GREEN ONION (including tops)
1 can (11 oz.) MANDARIN ORANGES
1 cup (1/2-inch cubes) SMOKED TURKEY
2/3 cup CALIFORNIA BING CHERRIES, washed and halved

Toss together all ingredients, except cherries, in a large bowl. Drizzle ***Balsamic Vinaigrette*** over salad, reserving 1 tablespoon of vinaigrette, and toss. Drizzle remaining vinaigrette over cherries and toss to coat. Arrange salad on individual plates and sprinkle with cherries.

Balsamic Vinaigrette

1/3 cup EXTRA-VIRGIN OLIVE OIL
2 Tbsp. BALSAMIC VINEGAR
1 Tbsp. STONE-GROUND MUSTARD
1 tsp. HONEY
SALT and freshly ground PEPPER to taste

In a bowl, whisk together all ingredients and refrigerate until ready to use.

Strawberry-Mango Salad

California Strawberry Commission—Watsonville

1 pint basket CALIFORNIA STRAWBERRIES, chopped
1 lg. MANGO, peeled and chopped
1/4 cup sliced GREEN ONIONS (including tops)
2 Tbsp. fresh LIME JUICE
1 Tbsp. chopped fresh CILANTRO
1/2 tsp. RED PEPPER FLAKES
1/4 tsp. CUMIN
SALT to taste

In a bowl, toss together all ingredients except salt and set aside for half an hour to allow flavors to blend. Mix in salt. Serve immediately or cover and refrigerate for up to two days.

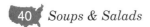

Tofu Dill Salad

"This can be served as a salad, spread on bread as a sand-wich filler or spread on hot toast as a topping."

Charlie Duke—Wildwood Harvest Foods, Watsonville

1 lb. WILDWOOD® FIRM TOFU
4 tsp. SAFFLOWER OIL
2 Tbsp. LEMON JUICE
2 tsp. APPLE CIDER VINEGAR
2 tsp. DILL
1 tsp. DRY MUSTARD
1 tsp. minced GARLIC
2/3 tsp. SEA SALT
1/2 tsp. CELERY SEED
1/4 lb. CELERY, finely chopped

In a food processor, combine all ingredients, except celery, and blend on low for 3 minutes. Pour tofu mixture into a bowl and fold in celery.

You're Talking Turkey in California!
More turkeys are raised in California than in any other state in the United States!

Turkey-Citrus Salad

Zacky Farms—South El Monte

3 Tbsp. OLIVE OIL
1 lb. ZACKY FARMS® TURKEY BREAST STRIPS
SALT and PEPPER to taste
1 head BIB LETTUCE, torn into bite-size pieces
2 cups BABY SPINACH, torn into bite-size pieces
1/2 cup HONEY MUSTARD DRESSING
2 med. ORANGES, cut into sections
2 med. GRAPEFRUIT, cut into sections
1 sm. RED ONION, cut into slivers
1 cup toasted PINE NUTS or chopped NUTS of choice

In a nonstick skillet, heat oil over medium-high heat and sauté turkey for 5 minutes or until tender and golden brown. Season with salt and pepper; let cool for 5 minutes. In a salad bowl, toss together lettuce, spinach and turkey with dressing. Arrange salad on plates and top each with orange and grape-fruit sections. Arrange onion slivers on top; sprinkle with nuts.

Almond Harvest Salad

Almond Board of California—Modesto

3 cups cooked WHITE and WILD RICE*
2 ORANGES, peeled and sectioned
1 APPLE, chopped
2 Tbsp. CURRANTS
1/4 cup finely diced RED ONIONS
2 cups cooked cubed CHICKEN BREAST
1/2 cup whole ALMONDS, toasted

In a mixing bowl, combine all ingredients. Toss with *Light Orange Dressing* and mix thoroughly. Chill at least 2-3 hours to allow flavors to blend before serving.

* May use 1 package (6 oz.) long grain and wild rice mix, omitting herb seasoning.

Light Orange Dressing

1/3 cup ALMOND or OLIVE OIL   2 tsp. LEMON JUICE
1/4 cup fresh ORANGE JUICE   1/4 tsp. SALT
1 Tbsp. fresh chopped PARSLEY   1/8 tsp. BLACK PEPPER

Combine all ingredients in mixing bowl. Whisk until thoroughly blended.

Toasted Tortilla Salad

MexGrocer.com (Recipe courtesy of Mission Foods)—La Jolla

4 CORN TORTILLAS   1/2 cup coarsely chopped
1 RED BELL PEPPER   CILANTRO LEAVES
1 POBLANO CHILE PEPPER   1 tsp. CHILI POWDER
5 GREEN ONIONS, thinly sliced   SALT to taste
2 CARROTS, shredded   1 Tbsp. OLIVE OIL
1/3 cup WHITE VINEGAR   2 cups SALAD GREENS
2 Tbsp. fresh LIME JUICE

Preheat oven to 400°. Slice the tortillas into very thin strips (1/8-inch or less). Place sliced tortillas on a baking sheet and toast until very crispy, about 8 minutes. Seed and thinly slice bell pepper and chile pepper. Combine vegetables in a mixing bowl with remaining ingredients. Add tortilla strips and toss just before serving.

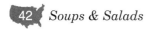

Beach Bundles

California Seafood Council—Sacramento

4 med. POTATOES, cooked, peeled and sliced
2 ONIONS, thickly sliced
1 lb. PACIFIC RED SNAPPER
SALT and PEPPER to taste
4 tsp. OLIVE OIL
4 cloves GARLIC, minced
JUICE of 1 LEMON
FRESH HERB SPRIGS: PARSLEY, DILL, TARRAGON or BASIL

Cut 8 (12-inch) squares of aluminum foil. Stack two squares of foil for each bundle. Brush top layers of foil with oil. Layer foil with potato, onion and then fish. Sprinkle with salt and pepper. In a bowl, combine olive oil, garlic and lemon juice and pour over top of fish. Add herb sprigs and fold foil to create a tight bundle. *Cook one of 3 ways:* 1. Bake at 325° for 20-30 minutes or until fish tests done. 2. Grill over very low, gray coals, turning frequently, until fish is done. 3. Wrap bundles in additional foil, place over hot rocks and coals in a pit at the beach and cover. Cook for an hour or until fish is done.

Tortilla-Chicken Casserole

Joseph Farms Cheese—Atwater

4 BONELESS, SKINLESS CHICKEN BREASTS
1 ONION, chopped
1 GREEN BELL PEPPER, chopped
1 tsp. minced GARLIC
1 pkg. (10-12 ct.) CORN TORTILLAS
2 cans (7 oz. ea.) DICED CHILES
2 cans (10.75 oz. ea.) CREAM OF CHICKEN SOUP
1 can (4.25 oz.) CHOPPED OLIVES
1 tsp. CHILI POWDER
1 tsp. CUMIN
1 lb. JOSEPH FARMS® CHEDDAR CHEESE, shredded
1 lb. JOSEPH FARMS® MONTEREY JACK CHEESE, shredded

In a saucepan, cover chicken with water and boil until tender. Add a small amount of chicken broth to a skillet; sauté onion, bell pepper and garlic until onion is translucent. Cut corn tortillas into bite-size pieces and soak them in remaining chicken broth. Shred chicken and place in a casserole dish; add sautéed vegetables and remaining ingredients and mix well. Bake at 350° for 30 minutes or until all cheese has melted.

San Francisco

Known as the "City by the Bay," San Francisco, with its clanging cable cars and steep and crooked streets, draws millions of tourists each year. Founded in 1776 by the Spanish, San Francisco became a busy mining supply center during the Gold Rush of 1849. In the late 1800s, it thrived as the financial and industrial capital of the West. In 1906, an earthquake and resulting fire destroyed most of the city. Today, this fascinating city has almost 800,000 residents and a diverse cultural makeup.

Pesce Al Cartoccio
(Fish Baked in Parchment)

"One of the simplest ways to cook moist, delicious fish is to cook it in parchment. These bundles can be prepared several hours ahead and refrigerated. Bring the fish back to room temperature before baking."

Biba Caggiano—Chef/Owner Biba Restaurant, Sacramento

4 (1/2 lb. ea.) SALMON or SEA BASS FILLETS
2-3 Tbsp. EXTRA VIRGIN OLIVE OIL
SALT and freshly ground PEPPER to taste
Juice of 1 LEMON
4 med. TOMATOES, sliced into 1/4-inch rounds
3 GREEN ONIONS, white parts only, diced
1 Tbsp. CAPERS, rinsed
6-8 fresh BASIL LEAVES, thinly shredded, or
     1 Tbsp. chopped fresh PARSLEY

Preheat oven to 400°. Cut 4 sheets of parchment paper* into 12 x 16-inch rectangles. Place the pieces of parchment paper on a work surface and brush lightly with oil. Place the fillets in the center of one half of each parchment sheet. Season the fish with salt and pepper and sprinkle with lemon juice. Top the fish with tomato slices, green onions, capers and basil and dribble with oil. Fold the other half of the parchment sheet over the fish and tightly fold edges to make a 1-inch border. Place parchment bundles on a baking sheet and bake 10-15 minutes, depending on the thickness of the fish (about 10 minutes per inch of thickness). At this point the fish should be cooked all the way through and the parchment should have puffed up and turned a dark brown color. Place each bundle on serving dishes and carefully unwrap or cut the parchment with a knife or scissors. Serve the fish in its own wrapping.

Serves 4.

*May use aluminum foil if desired.

Pizza Rustica

Mike Gallo—Joseph Farms Cheese, Atwater

8 oz. JOSEPH FARMS® MOZZARELLA CHEESE, diced
1 carton (15 oz.) RICOTTA CHEESE
2/3 cup grated PARMESAN CHEESE
1 1/2 cups cooked diced HAM
1/8 tsp. PEPPER
3/4 tsp. SALT
1 pkg. (10 oz.) frozen CHOPPED SPINACH, thawed
2 EGGS
2 1/3 cups FLOUR
1 Tbsp. SUGAR
1/2 tsp. SALT
3/4 cup MARGARINE
4 Tbsp. ICE WATER
4 HARD-BOILED EGGS, peeled and sliced

In large bowl, stir together mozzarella, ricotta and Parmesan cheeses, ham, pepper and 1/4 tsp. salt . Drain spinach in strainer, pressing out as much liquid as possible. Separate 1 egg, reserving yolk. Stir egg white, 1 remaining egg and spinach into cheese mixture. In a separate bowl, sift together flour, sugar and 1/2 tsp. salt. Cut in margarine with a pastry blender until mixture is coarsely crumbled. Mix reserved yolk with 3 tablespoons ice water. Sprinkle yolk mixture and remaining ice water over crumb mixture, tossing with a fork until dough forms. Press dough firmly into a ball. On a lightly floured surface, roll out 2/3 of dough to a 15-inch square; fit into bottom and up the sides of 8 x 8 baking dish. Trim pastry to 1 inch beyond edge of dish. Gather scraps and roll out with remaining dough to a 12-inch square. Spread 1/2 of the cheese mixture in bottom of pastry-lined baking dish. Arrange hard-boiled egg slices on top of cheese layer. Spread with remaining cheese mixture. Place 12-inch pastry square on top and trim to 1 inch beyond edge of dish. Fold edge of top pastry under edge of bottom pastry and flute. Cut slits in top crust to vent. Bake in 375° oven for 50 minutes or until crust is golden and filling is bubbly. Cool on rack. Serve at room temperature or chilled.

Pineapple Sugar Shrimp

Contessa Food Products—San Pedro

2 cups PINEAPPLE CHUNKS
1 RED BELL PEPPER, seeded and diced
1 GREEN BELL PEPPER, seeded and diced
2 JALAPEÑO PEPPERS, seeded and diced
1 1/2 Tbsp. fresh minced GINGERROOT
12 oz. EXTRA JUMBO 21/25 CONTESSA® UNCOOKED TAIL-ON
   SHRIMP, thawed and drained
1/4 cup packed BROWN SUGAR
2 Tbsp. LEMON JUICE
1/4 lb. BUTTER, cut into pieces

Preheat grill. Cut 4 pieces of aluminum foil (12 x 12-inches each). Place 1/4 cup of pineapple in the center of each piece of foil. In a bowl, mix together all peppers wih gingerroot and place on top of pineapple. Place shrimp on top of pepper mixture. In a small bowl, mix together brown sugar and lemon juice; sprinkle on top of shrimp. Top with butter pieces. Fold the aluminum foil to make an enclosed packet, leaving room for heat circulation. Place packets on grill and cook for 8-10 minutes. Serve over rice.

Downtown San Francisco

Here you will find the Civic Center, which includes City Hall, the War Memorial Opera House and the Asian Art Museum. Nob Hill and its luxury hotels are nearby. Just east lies Chinatown's colorful shops and restaurants that stretch for eight blocks. Further east are the financial district's 48-story Transamerica Pyramid and the 52-story Bank of America building.

Pecan Smoked Raspberry-Chipotle Beef Tenderloin

Chef James Howard—Oceanside

4-5 lbs. WHOLE BEEF TENDERLOIN, trimmed and tied about every 2 inches

Raspberry-Chipotle Marinade:
1/2 cup RASPBERRY PRESERVES
1/2 cup fresh RASPBERRIES
2 Tbsp. APPLE CIDER VINEGAR
1 CHIPOTLE PEPPER
1 clove GARLIC
1/2 tsp. SALT (optional)

Dry Rub:
1/3 cup GRILL MATES® MONTREAL STEAK SEASONING
1 Tbsp. whole CUMIN SEED
1 Tbsp. freshly cracked BLACK PEPPER
1/2 Tbsp. dried THYME

In food processor, combine all of the marinade ingredients and process until smooth. In a bowl, mix all dry rub ingredients. Cover and set aside. Place beef tenderloin and marinate in a large Ziplock® bag and refrigerate overnight. When ready to prepare, place beef tenderloin on a large cookie sheet and sprinkle with dry rub. Cook on the grill with your favorite soaked wood chips (I prefer pecan chips) using indirect method, about 15 minutes per pound or until internal temperature reaches 130°. Let beef rest for 20 minutes before cutting.

More Than A Sunday Drive

The scenic 17-Mile Drive between Monterey and Carmel offers motorists a wide range of delightful sights and experiences. Those who pull over at Seal Rock will catch a glimpse of the social habits of harbor seals. Other must-sees include Shepherd's Knoll, with its panoramic view of the bay, and Pescadero Point, the place to witness some of the most breathtaking sunsets on the West Coast.

Gourmet Crab & Avocado Enchiladas

California Avocado Commission—Santa Ana

1 cup MILD SALSA
1 cup SOUR CREAM
1/4 cup chopped fresh CILANTRO
1/2 cup minced GREEN ONIONS
1 cup shredded MONTEREY JACK CHEESE
1/4 tsp. SALT
8 oz. LUMP CRAB MEAT
4 (8-inch) FLOUR TORTILLAS
1 AVOCADO, 1/2 diced and 1/2 sliced
3/4 cup RED ENCHILADA SAUCE
1 TOMATO, diced

Preheat oven to 400°. In a bowl, combine salsa, 1/2 cup sour cream, cilantro, green onions, 1/2 cup shredded cheese, salt and crab meat; stir gently. Spray a 13 x 9 baking pan with non-stick cooking spray. Lay 1 tortilla on a flat surface and spread 1/4 of the filling in a line down the center. Place some of the diced avocado on top of the filling, roll up the tortilla and place it seam-side down in the pan. Repeat with the remaining tortillas and filling. Pour enchilada sauce over all and sprinkle with the remaining cheese. Bake 15-18 minutes or until lightly browned and bubbling. Top with the sliced avocado and remaining sour cream. Sprinkle with tomato and remaining green onions.

Alcatraz Island

This island in San Francisco Bay, known as "The Rock," is one of San Francisco's most famous landmarks. Originally a military fortress, then prison (some Civil War prisoners were housed here), Alcatraz was a federal prison from 1933 to 1963. Famous prisoners included Al Capone, "Machine Gun" Kelly and Robert "The Birdman of Alcatraz" Stroud.

Coq au Vin

Courtesy Julius Orth—deLorimier Winery, Geyserville

6 CHICKEN LEGS and THIGHS
2 cups BEEF BOUILLON
SALT and PEPPER to taste
1 Tbsp. VEGETABLE OIL
3 Tbsp. BUTTER
4 slices BACON
12 oz. MUSHROOMS, quartered
1 1/2 cups PEARL ONIONS
2 Tbsp. ALL-PURPOSE FLOUR

Add chicken to **Wine Marinade** and marinate overnight in refrigerator. Strain ingredients from marinade, reserving vegetables, and pour marinade into a large pot. Add beef bouillon and slowly bring to a simmer. Separate chicken legs and thighs; pat dry and sprinkle lightly with salt & pepper. In a skillet, heat vegetable oil and butter and fry bacon until brown and crispy; remove and set aside. Sauté chicken in bacon drippings, turning once, until skin is lightly browned, about 10 minutes. Add chicken to the pot. Add marinade vegetables to skillet and sauté on medium-high for about 7 minutes; add to pot. Simmer mixture for approximately 1 hour. In the same skillet, sauté mushrooms and pearl onions until tender, about 10 minutes; add to pot. Deglaze skillet with a splash of the reserved wine and add to pot. In a small bowl, combine flour with remaining wine. Remove pot from heat; whisk in flour mixture. Return to heat and simmer, stirring regularly, until mixture has thickened. Crumble bacon and add to pot; simmer 10 more minutes.

Serves 6.

Wine Marinade

1 bottle (750 ml) deLORIMIER®
    MERLOT
2 med. CARROTS, sliced
2 ONIONS, chopped

3 stalks CELERY, chopped
1 tsp. fresh THYME
2 BAY LEAVES

Combine marinade ingredients in a nonmetallic container, reserving 1/2 cup of wine.

Ranchero Grilled Salmon Steak with Roasted Corn-Black Bean Salsa

California King Salmon Council—Folsom

Citrus Marinade:
- 1/2 cup fresh ORANGE JUICE
- 1/4 cup fresh LIME JUICE
- 2 Tbsp. OLIVE OIL
- 2 cloves GARLIC, crushed
- 1 SERRANO CHILE, seeded and minced
- 2 tsp. grated LIME PEEL
- 1/2 tsp. SALT
- 1/8 tsp. coarsely ground BLACK PEPPER

4 (6 oz. ea.) CALIFORNIA KING SALMON® STEAKS

In a small bowl, whisk together marinade ingredients. Reserving 1/3 cup marinade for the salsa, pour marinade over the salmon in a self-sealing plastic bag and refrigerate for 30 minutes. Place the salmon on an oiled grill 4 inches from medium-hot coals. Grill about 5 minutes per side, brushing with marinade from time to time. Salmon is done when the meat is evenly colored and flakes easily. Serve with *Roasted Corn-Black Bean Salsa*.

Roasted Corn-Black Bean Salsa

- 3-4 EARS fresh CORN ON THE COB (husks removed)
- 1 can (15 oz.) BLACK BEANS, rinsed
- 2 ROMA TOMATOES, diced
- 1/3 cup GREEN ONIONS, minced
- 1/3 cup fresh CILANTRO, minced
- 2 SERRANO CHILES, seeded and minced
- 1/2 tsp. SALT
- 1/2 tsp. CHILI POWDER
- 1/4 tsp. ground BLACK PEPPER

Roast ears of corn on grill until cooked and golden brown, 5-10 minutes. Cool. Slice kernels off the cobs and place in a bowl. Gently stir in all remaining ingredients, adding reserved marinade. Refrigerate until ready to serve.

Grilled California Seafood Tacos with Corn Salsa

California Seafood Council—Sacramento

1 lb. CALIFORNIA ROCKFISH FILLETS*
JUICE of 2 LIMES
2 tsp. OLIVE OIL
8 fresh CORN TORTILLAS

Marinate fillets in lime juice and olive oil for 1/2 hour. Grill fish 2-3 minutes per side or until it flakes easily. In a 200° oven or in a skillet over low heat, warm tortillas until pliable. Place two tortillas on serving plates so that they halfway overlap each other. Place fish in center and add **Corn Salsa** and other garnishes to taste. Roll tacos up and skewer with toothpicks to hold together.

Serves 4.

*California halibut, shark, barracuda, bonito, Spanish mackerel or tuna may be used.

Corn Salsa

1 cup cooked CORN
1 med. RED ONION, chopped
1 cup seeded, chopped CUCUMBER
2 JALAPEÑO PEPPERS, minced
1/2 bunch fresh CILANTRO, chopped
SALT and PEPPER to taste
JUICE of 2 LIMES

In a bowl, combine all salsa ingredients.

The Crookedest Street in the World!

A section of Lombard Street which ascends Russian Hill in San Francisco, makes 8 sharp turns in a single block!

Calypso Coconut Chicken with Mango-Peach Marmalade

California Poultry Federation—Modesto

3/4 cup FLOUR
1 tsp. SALT
1 tsp. GINGER
1/4 tsp. CAYENNE PEPPER
1 cup SWEETENED SHREDDED
   COCONUT
1 cup PANKO BREAD CRUMBS

2 EGGS
2 Tbsp. SOY SAUCE
1 1/4 lbs. CHICKEN BREAST
   TENDERS
3 Tbsp. VEGETABLE OIL
CILANTRO SPRIGS

In a shallow dish, combine flour, salt, ginger and cayenne pepper. In another shallow dish, combine coconut and panko bread crumbs. In a small bowl, whisk eggs with soy sauce. Dredge chicken in flour mixture, dip in egg mixture and coat with coconut mixture, pressing to adhere. Heat oil in a nonstick skillet over medium-high heat. Add chicken and sauté 3-4 minutes per side or until golden brown and cooked through. Garnish with cilantro and serve with *Mango-Peach Marmalade* on the side.

Serves 4.

Mango-Peach Marmalade

1 MANGO, peeled and diced
2 PEACHES, peeled and diced
1/4 cup SUGAR
1 1/2 tsp. minced JALAPEÑO PEPPER
1 Tbsp. fresh LEMON JUICE
1 tsp. RICE VINEGAR
2 Tbsp. chopped fresh CILANTRO

In a small saucepan, combine mango, peaches, sugar, jalapeño, lemon juice and vinegar. Simmer over medium-low heat for 20 minutes, stirring occasionally. Remove from heat and stir in cilantro. Refrigerate or serve at room temperature.

Home-Baked Tofu

Carroll Rosenmayr—Wildwood Harvest Foods, Watsonville

Marinade:

1/4 cup OLIVE OIL	1 cup COOKING SHERRY
1/4 cup TOASTED SESAME OIL	or MIRIN
3 Tbsp. minced GARLIC	1 Tbsp. HONEY (optional)
4 oz. GINGERROOT, pressed	1/2 Tbsp. ROSEMARY
1/2 cup RICE VINEGAR	1/2 Tbsp. OREGANO
1/2 cup LEMON JUICE	1/2 Tbsp. BASIL
1 cup TAMARI	1/2 Tbsp. DILL WEED

2 lbs. WILDWOOD® FIRM NIGARI TOFU
1 RED ONION, sliced into rings
3 Tbsp. ARROWROOT
3 1/2 cups WATER

In a small skillet, heat oils and sauté garlic and ginger for 1 minute. Pour into a bowl. Add remaining marinade ingredients and whisk well. (If using fresh herbs, increase to 1 tablespoon of each.) Slice tofu into 3/4-inch slices and place in a shallow pan or baking dish. Pour marinade over tofu and marinate for 1 hour, turning every 15 minutes. Remove tofu and place in a large skillet. Add 3 cups of the water to marinade and pour over tofu; place onion rings on top. Bring mixture to a boil; reduce heat, cover and simmer for 10 minutes. Remove tofu from skillet and place on a baking pan lined with parchment paper. Bake at 350° for 12 minutes. While tofu bakes, remove onion from the marinade and set aside. Strain marinade and pour back into skillet. In a small bowl, mix arrowroot with remaining water and stir until dissolved. Add to marinade and slowly bring mixture to a boil, whisking constantly, until thickened. Remove tofu from oven and flip; return to oven and bake for an additional 10 minutes. Remove from oven and place an onion ring on top of each slice of tofu, drizzle with 1 tablespoon of marinade and bake for an additional 5 minutes.

Coit Tower

This famous San Francisco landmark, a memorial to the city's firefighters, stands on top of Telegraph Hill.

Avocado Stuffed Chicken Breasts

California Avocado Commission—Santa Ana

4 CHICKEN BREASTS, pounded flat
2 AVOCADOS, peeled and sliced
3 Tbsp. LIME JUICE
1 tsp. LEMON PEPPER
1 tsp. GARLIC POWDER
1/2 cup minced fresh BASIL LEAVES
1 lg. TOMATO, seeded & diced
1/2 cup SWEET ONION, chopped
2 Tbsp. CRACKED PEPPERCORNS

Place chicken breasts on a flat surface. In a bowl, mix together all remaining ingredients, except peppercorns. Spread 1/2 of the avocado mixture onto chicken breasts and roll up, tucking in ends. Cover and refrigerate remaining avocado mixture. Place breasts in a lightly oiled baking dish and sprinkle with peppercorns. Bake at 350° for 45 minutes or until chicken is fork tender. Remove from oven. Cut each breast in half and arrange on a platter with the remaining avocado mixture. Garnish with fresh basil, lime slices, small tomatoes and avocado slices (or any combination of these).

Serves 4.

San Francisco's Famous Bridges

Two spectacular bridges link San Francisco to other parts of the Bay Area. The Golden Gate Bridge, which has a total length of almost 9,000 feet, stretches northward and is one of the world's longest single-span suspension bridges. The 8.4-mile (4.5 over water) San Francisco-Oakland Bay Bridge links San Francisco with the East Bay cities.

Golden Gate Bridge

Kristina's Clam Spaghetti with Gremolata

"My family has passed this clam spaghetti recipe down for generations. I have improved it with the addition of fresh basil and lemon."

Kristina Tellefsen—Santa Nella House Bed & Breakfast, Guerneville

1 lb. SPAGHETTI
2 tsp. SALT (optional)
1 tsp. OLIVE OIL
2 cans (6 oz. ea.) MINCED CLAMS

Clam Sauce:
1/4 cup OLIVE OIL
3 lg. cloves GARLIC, minced
1 bottle (8 oz.) CLAM JUICE
2 tsp. dried BASIL
2 Tbsp. dried PARSLEY

1/2 tsp. freshly ground
   BLACK PEPPER
1/4 cup fresh LEMON JUICE
1/4 cup WHITE WINE

In a large pot, cook spaghetti in salted water until *al dente* according to the directions on the package; drain and toss with oil. Drain clams, reserving juice. Heat oil in a skillet and sauté garlic for 1 minute; *do not allow garlic to brown.* Stir in reserved clam juice, bottled clam juice, basil, parsley and pepper. Boil vigorously for 3 minutes or until sauce has reduced slightly. Add lemon juice and wine. Cook another minute to evaporate the alcohol; remove from heat. Add clams and stir well. Place pasta in bowls and top with clam sauce. Sprinkle generously with **Gremolata.** Garnish with Parmesan cheese if desired.

Serves 4.

Gremolata

3 Tbsp. BREAD CRUMBS
3 Tbsp. grated PARMESAN CHEESE
2 Tbsp. finely chopped, fresh PARSLEY
3 Tbsp. finely julienned, fresh BASIL
1 clove GARLIC, crushed or minced
Grated PEEL of 1 LEMON

In a small bowl, combine all ingredients and mix well.

Grilled Tenderloin of Pork with Truffle Marinade and Oregon Blue Cheese Cream Sauce

Chef Stephen Smith—Albion River Inn, Albion

1 (1 lb.) PORK TENDERLOIN

Oregon Blue Cheese Cream Sauce:
    2 oz. BUTTER
    12 SHIITAKE MUSHROOMS, sliced
    1 Tbsp. GARLIC, minced
    1 Tbsp. SHALLOTS, minced
    2 oz. SEASONED RICE WINE VINEGAR
    2 oz. VEAL STOCK
    2 oz. HEAVY CREAM
    4 oz. OREGON BLUE CHEESE

Place pork in a nonmetallic pan, add *Truffle Marinade* and turn to cover all sides; marinate for 30 minutes. Meanwhile, in a large skillet, heat butter until golden brown. Add mushrooms, garlic and shallots and sauté for 2 minutes. Stir in rice wine vinegar and reduce until almost dry. Add the veal stock and heavy cream and reduce by half. Crumble blue cheese into sauce and simmer gently for 2-3 minutes. Set sauce aside and keep warm. Remove pork from marinade and place on preheated grill. Cook for 12-15 minutes, turning to grill evenly on all sides. Remove from grill and let rest for 5 minutes. Thinly slice pork, fan on plates and spoon sauce over top.

Serves 4.

Truffle Marinade

1 oz. WHITE TRUFFLE OIL
2 oz. RASPBERRY VINEGAR
1 oz. SOY SAUCE

2 Tbsp. minced GARLIC
2 Tbsp. minced SHALLOTS
SALT and PEPPER to taste

In a bowl, combine marinade ingredients.

Chicken Breast
with Fennel & Tomatoes

This dish is super when served on a bed of orzo pasta
sprinkled with feta cheese.

California Tomato Commission—Fresno

4 BONELESS, SKINLESS CHICKEN BREASTS, split
1 tsp. SALT
1/4 tsp. BLACK PEPPER
3 Tbsp. OLIVE OIL
1 Tbsp. crushed FENNEL SEED
1/2-1 tsp. crushed RED CHILE FLAKES
2 Tbsp. minced GARLIC
2 FENNEL BULBS (3 cups), sliced 1/2-inch thick
6 cups diced CALIFORNIA TOMATOES
JUICE and grated PEEL of 2 LEMONS
1 cup pitted KALAMATA OLIVES
2 Tbsp. minced fresh ITALIAN PARSLEY

Season chicken with salt and pepper. In a heavy saucepan, heat oil and sear chicken for about 3-5 minutes on each side, until golden brown. Add fennel seed, chile flakes and garlic. Cook for 1 minute and stir in fennel, tomato, lemon juice and grated peel. Cover and reduce heat to medium. Cook for 10 minutes or until tomato mixture thickens slightly. Add olives and parsley. Cook, uncovered, for an additional 10-15 minutes, until sauce has thickened and chicken is thoroughly cooked.

Serves 4.

Transportation in the Bay Area

The San Francisco International Airport (SFO) currently handles over 40 million passengers each year on more than 30 different airlines, making it one of the world's busiest. The publicly owned BART (Bay Area Rapid Transit), a 71-mile electric rail system, serves much of the Bay region. One route is through the Transbay Tube, a tunnel under the San Francisco Bay between San Francisco and Oakland.

Burgers with Raisin Salsa

California Raisins Marketing Board—Fresno

Raisin Salsa:
  5 PLUM TOMATOES, diced
  1 Tbsp. finely chopped GREEN ONIONS
  1/2 cup chopped CALIFORNIA RAISINS
  2 Tbsp. chopped fresh BASIL
  1 Tbsp. OLIVE OIL
  1 Tbsp. BALSAMIC VINEGAR
  BLACK PEPPER to taste

1-1/2 pounds GROUND ROUND

Prepare grill. In a small bowl, combine salsa ingredients and set aside. Shape beef into 8 patties. Make a small indentation in the center of 4 patties. Spoon 1 tablespoon of salsa into each indentation. Top with remaining patties. Seal sides well. Grill burgers 3-4 inches above hot coals until done (160° at thickest part). Place burgers on toasted buns and top with remaining salsa.

Did You Know?
At least two communities, Selma and Fresno, lay claim to being called the Raisin Capital of the World!

Avocado Wrap

An alternative to sandwiches for a light, healthy lunch.

California Avocado Commission—Santa Ana

HUMMUS (your favorite flavor)
1 HABANERO BURRITO TORTILLA
  (or plain if desired)
3-4 thin slices SMOKED TURKEY
  BREAST

3 slices SWISS CHEESE
ALFALFA SPROUTS
1/2 TOMATO, chopped
1 CALIFORNIA AVOCADO
SALT and PEPPER to taste

Spread hummus thinly over the entire tortilla. Layer turkey and cheese over 1/2 of the area. Place vegetables and slices of avocado in a narrow vertical line centered on top of the meat and cheese. Sprinkle salt and pepper over all. Roll tortilla tightly and secure with toothpicks.

Pan Seared Striped Sea Bass with Orange-Basil Cream Sauce

A quick and delicious meal that is perfect for summer entertaining.

Domaine Carneros—Napa

2 (6 oz. ea.) portions STRIPED
   SEA BASS
SALT and PEPPER to taste
2 Tbsp. OLIVE OIL
1 Tbsp. BUTTER
1 med. SHALLOT, diced
1 lg. clove GARLIC, minced
1 cup DRY WHITE WINE

JUICE of 1 ORANGE
Pinch of CUMIN
6 oz. HEAVY CREAM
SALT and PEPPER to taste
Fresh LEMON JUICE
6 lg. BASIL LEAVES, thinly
   sliced (reserve stems)

Pat sea bass dry and sprinkle with salt and pepper. In a skillet, heat olive oil until just smoking. Sear fish for 2-3 minutes per side or until golden and crispy. Place fish in an ovenproof dish and bake at 400° for approximately 8 minutes. In a stainless steel pan, melt butter and sauté shallot and garlic until just beginning to brown. Add wine and orange juice and reduce until syrupy. Add a pinch of cumin, reserved basil stems and heavy cream and simmer very gently until reduced by 1/3. Adjust the sauce with salt, pepper and a few drops of lemon juice (this must be done after the sauce has been reduced to avoid curdling). Strain sauce and serve over fish. Sprinkle with basil. Accompany with garlic mashed potatoes, green beans with slivered sun-dried tomatoes and Domaine Carneros® Blanc de Blancs.

San Francisco's Cable Cars
Andrew Smith Hallidie tested the world's first cable car here in 1873. To learn more about the cable cars, visit the Cable Car Museum on Mason Street.

Pasta with Peperonata Sauce

*"Roasting peppers is not necessary, but it enhances
the flavor wonderfully."*

Susan Foppiano Valera—Foppiano Vineyards, Healdsburg

3 qts. WATER
1 Tbsp. OLIVE OIL
1 Tbsp. SALT
1 pkg. (12 oz.) WHOLE-WHEAT SPAGHETTI or LINGUINI
1 Tbsp. CAPERS (optional)
1/4 cup grated PARMESAN CHEESE

In a saucepan, bring 3 quarts of water to a boil; add oil, salt and pasta and cook according to directions on package; drain. Gently mix pasta with ***Peperonata Sauce***, capers and Parmesan cheese. Serve immediately.

Serves 4.

Suggested wine: Foppiano® Zinfandel.

Peperonata Sauce

4 lg. or 6 med. BELL PEPPERS,
**   red, green and yellow**
1 lg. WHITE ONION, slivered
2-3 cloves GARLIC, crushed
1/4 cup OLIVE OIL

1 lb. TOMATOES, quartered
1 Tbsp. fresh BASIL
**   LEAVES, chopped**
1/3 cup RED WINE
SALT to taste

Roast peppers under a broiler or over a gas flame until skin blackens. Place in a paper bag for a few minutes; then remove and peel under running water. Cut peppers into thin strips. Meanwhile, in a skillet, sauté onion and garlic in olive oil until soft; add peppers and continue to cook, stirring often, for a few more minutes. Purée mixture in blender and return to skillet. In a saucepan, cook tomatoes over low heat until soft; pass through a food mill or strainer and add to pepper mixture. Add basil, wine and salt and cook another 10-15 minutes over medium heat, stirring often, until sauce is reduced to 3 cups.

Pumpkin Ravioli with Walnut Sauce

Chris Lewand—Camellia Cellars, Healdsburg

Walnut Sauce:
3/4 cup shelled WALNUTS
1/4 cup PIGNOLI (pine nuts)
1/2 tsp. MARJORAM
3 Tbsp. OLIVE OIL

1/2 cup RICOTTA CHEESE
Dash of NUTMEG
SALT and freshly ground
 PEPPER to taste

White Sauce:
2 Tbsp. BUTTER
2 Tbsp. FLOUR
1 cup MILK

SALT and PEPPER to taste
Dash of NUTMEG

PUMPKIN RAVIOLI
1/2 cup HEAVY CREAM

To make walnut sauce: In a wooden bowl, mash together walnuts and pignoli to a grainy consistency. Add remaining sauce ingredients and stir to mix; set aside. To make white sauce: In a saucepan, heat butter to bubbling. Add flour and whisk until blended. In a separate pan, scald milk and then whisk quickly into flour and butter until smooth. Stir and cook over low heat for about 10 minutes; add seasonings. Combine the sauces, adding cream to desired consistency. In a saucepan, cook ravioli according to directions on package; drain. Pour sauce over ravioli and gently stir to coat.

Golden Gate National Recreation Area

This national park protects many areas throughout the San Francisco Bay area, from the beaches to the peaks of the Marin Headlands and the old-growth coast redwood forest of Muir Woods National Monument. In 1908, Muir Woods was named for John Muir who founded the Sierra Club and was instrumental in the establishment of both the Yosemite and Sequoia National Parks. The tallest trees in Muir Woods are about 260 feet high and 600-800 years old.

Muir Woods

Vegetable Lasagna

Rhonda Carano—Ferrari-Carano Vineyards and Winery,
Healdsburg

1 lb. LASAGNA NOODLES
1 lb. RICOTTA CHEESE
2 cups shredded MOZZARELLA CHEESE
1/2 tsp. each SALT and PEPPER
1/2 cup chopped fresh BASIL
3/4 cup PARMESAN CHEESE
1/2 tsp. NUTMEG
1 EGG
1 pkg. (10 oz.) frozen chopped SPINACH, thawed and
    squeezed dry
2 Tbsp. OLIVE OIL
3 ZUCCHINI, sliced 1/4-inch thick
1 med. JAPANESE EGGPLANT, sliced 1/2-inch thick
1 lb. fresh MUSHROOMS, sliced thinly
1 qt. MARINARA SAUCE
3 cups BÉCHAMEL SAUCE (your favorite recipe)

Grease a 13 x 9 baking pan. Cook lasagna noodles according to directions on package; drain and layer between sheets of parchment paper. In a bowl, mix the next 9 ingredients together. Set aside. Lightly brush zucchini and eggplant slices with olive oil, season with salt and pepper and grill over coals (or quickly sear in a non-stick skillet). Add olive oil to a skillet and sauté mushrooms over high heat. Season lightly with salt and pepper and cook until juices have evaporated. Spread half of the marinara sauce on the bottom of the baking pan. Arrange one-third of the noodles over the sauce and spread with half of the ricotta cheese mixture. Top with half of the grilled vegetables and mushrooms. Spread all of the béchamel sauce over the vegetables. Layer with another one-third of the noodles. Spread the remaining ricotta mixture over noodles and top with remaining vegetables. Arrange the last of the noodles on top and spread with the rest of the marinara sauce. Cover pan with with heavy-duty aluminum foil. Bake at 350° for 1 hour or until bubbly. Uncover and let stand 15 minutes before cutting.

Serves 10.

Grilled Wasabi Tuna with Vegetable Tempura

Ikedas California Country Market—Auburn

6 (8 oz.) TUNA FILLETS
EXTRA VIRGIN OLIVE OIL
Fine SEA SALT
Freshly ground BLACK PEPPER
SOY SAUCE
IKEDAS® CREAMY WASABI SAUCE
Cooked JASMINE or SHORT-GRAIN WHITE RICE

Preheat grill to a very high temperature. Season tuna with olive oil, salt and pepper. Place tuna on grill for 30 seconds and then turn 90 degrees for 30 more seconds (for nice grill marks). Flip tuna and cook a few more seconds, until slightly pink in the middle. Pour wasabi sauce onto half of each plate and drizzle soy sauce in a zigzag fashion over top. Place a fillet on top of sauce and add *Vegetable Tempura* and hot rice to remaining half of plate.

Serves 6.

Vegetable Tempura

VEGETABLE OIL for cooking
Your choice of VEGETABLES*, thinly sliced

Batter:
   1 cup COLD WATER (40° is a must or tempura will be oily)
   2 EGGS, beaten
   1 cup FLOUR
   2 Tbsp. DRY WHITE WINE

Heat oil to 340° in a deep, thick-walled pan or wok. Place water in a bowl and add eggs, flour and wine. Whisk quickly and mix evenly. Dip veggies in batter and place carefully in oil. Remove from oil when the batter turns *slightly* brown.

*Green beans, onions, bell peppers, broccoli, zucchini, carrots, etc.

Asian Spring Asparagus

California Pistachio Commission—Fresno

1 lb. fresh ASPARAGUS
1 Tbsp. VEGETABLE OIL
1/4 tsp. GROUND GINGER
1/4 tsp. BLACK PEPPER
1 Tbsp. SOY SAUCE
1/3 cup coarsely chopped CALIFORNIA PISTACHIOS

Trim woody ends of asparagus spears. Slice asparagus (with a sharp diagonal slant) into 3-inch lengths. Heat oil in a large skillet until a piece of asparagus sizzles. Add asparagus, ginger and pepper; stir-fry over medium-high heat for 2 minutes. Add soy sauce and stir-fry 2 minutes longer. Add pistachios and stir-fry briefly just to heat through

Serves 4.

California Pistachios
Approximately 98% of the United States pistachio crop is grown in California!

Artichokes, Hot off the Grill

There's nothing like a good old-fashioned barbeque!
Grilled marinated artichokes can be a perfect
accompaniment to virtually any meal.

Capurro Marketing, LLC—Moss Landing

4 lg. TOPLESS™ GLOBE ARTICHOKES

Marinade:
1/2 cup ROASTED GARLIC TERIYAKI SAUCE
1/2 cup BALSAMIC VINEGAR
1/2 cup OLIVE OIL
2 Tbsp. chopped GARLIC
2 Tbsp. minced GINGERROOT

Slice 1/3 of artichoke tops off crosswise. Trim stems, cut off thorns and discard lower leaves. Rinse under cold running water. Boil or steam artichokes* until bottoms pierce easily with a sharp knife, about 30 minutes. Drain artichokes and cool. Cut each artichoke in half lengthwise and then in half again, making 4 quarters. Cut out the fuzzy center along with any purple-tipped petals. In a large bowl, combine marinade ingredients. Add artichokes to marinade, coating all sides. Marinate artichokes at least 1 hour or overnight. Remove artichokes, reserving marinade, and place cut-side down on a grill over a solid bed of medium coals or on a gas grill over medium heat. Grill until lightly browned on the cut side, about 5 minutes. Turn over and grill until petals are slightly charred. Warm marinade and serve as a dip or sauce.

*Artichokes can be cooked on the grill instead of boiled or steamed. Trim, quarter and marinate uncooked artichokes as directed above. Place two 1/4-inch wedges on a piece of foil, folding over and sealing edges to make a sealed pouch. Repeat with remaining artichokes. Grill for about 20 minutes, until a knife inserts easily into the heart of the artichoke. Remove from foil and grill as directed.

Harvest Vegetable Platter with Orange-Walnut Sauce

California Walnut Commission—Sacramento

1 ACORN SQUASH, halved, seeded and cut into 1/4-inch thick slices
2 cups BROCCOLI FLORETS and sliced STEMS
2 cups CAULIFLOWER FLORETS
2 cups CARROTS, cut in 1/4-inch slices

Arrange acorn squash slices in overlapping pattern around the outside edge of a large microwaveable platter. Arrange a row of broccoli next to the squash, then a row of cauliflower. Place sliced carrots in the center. Cover with plastic wrap, venting one corner. Microwave on High 8-10 minutes, turning twice, until vegetables are tender but still crisp. Let stand 5 minutes. Pour off any liquid from platter. Pour ***Orange-Walnut Sauce*** over vegetables and serve.

Orange-Walnut Sauce

1/2 cup BUTTER
1/4 cup FROZEN ORANGE JUICE CONCENTRATE
2 Tbsp. DIJON MUSTARD
4 Tbsp. minced GREEN ONION
1/4 tsp. RED PEPPER FLAKES (optional)
3/4 cup chopped CALIFORNIA WALNUTS

Place butter, orange juice concentrate, mustard, green onion and red pepper flakes in a glass dish. Microwave on High for 2 minutes or until butter is melted. Add walnuts and stir until combined.

Note: Sauce may be made up to 3 days ahead and refrigerated in a sealed container. To reheat, microwave 2 minutes on High and stir before serving.

Rodeo Time!

Every April, Red Bluff, a small town just south of Redding, hosts one of the top rodeos in America!

Mamaw's Eggplant

Margit F. Chiriaco-Rusche—Joseph L. Chiriaco Inc., Chiriaco
Summit

1 EGGPLANT, peeled and sliced
1 ONION, chopped
1 cup sliced MUSHROOMS
1 cup sliced TOMATOES or 1 can (16 oz.) diced TOMATOES
1/2 lb. MONTEREY JACK, MOZZARELLA or CHEDDAR
    CHEESE, shredded
1/4 cup sliced, pitted GREEN OLIVES

Generously oil a casserole dish. Layer eggplant, onion,
mushrooms and tomato. Sprinkle with cheese and olives. Bake
at 350° for 45 minutes or until eggplant is cooked through and
tender.

Note: If desired, add topping of croutons or Italian bread crumbs.

Sunset Peach Salsa

California Cling Peach Board, Dinuba

1 can (15 oz.) CALIFORNIA CLING PEACH SLICES
4 tsp. WHITE WINE VINEGAR
4 tsp. LIME JUICE
2 tsp. finely grated LIME PEEL
3 Tbsp. chopped fresh MINT
1/4 cup chopped fresh CORIANDER
1/4 tsp. each SALT and PEPPER
1 Tbsp. OLIVE OIL
3/4 cup diced PINEAPPLE, drained
1/2 cup chopped ORANGE SEGMENTS
1/2 cup finely chopped ENGLISH CUCUMBER
1/3 cup finely chopped RED ONION
3 Tbsp. seeded and finely chopped JALAPEÑO PEPPERS

Drain peaches; dice into small pieces and set aside. In a
large bowl, combine vinegar, lime juice, lime peel, mint, coriander, pepper and salt. Whisk mixture while adding oil. Add
peach slices and remaining ingredients. Stir gently until well-
mixed. Cover and refrigerate until ready to serve.

Cheesy Broccoli Casserole

"This recipe is a family favorite—everyone likes it. Fresh broccoli is always available in southern California."

Carol Palluth—Oak Glen Curio Shop, Yucaipa

1 1/2 lbs. BROCCOLI
2 EGGS, lightly beaten
3/4 cup COTTAGE CHEESE
1/2 cup shredded CHEDDAR CHEESE
2 Tbsp. finely chopped ONION
1 tsp. WORCESTERSHIRE SAUCE
1/2 tsp. SALT
1/8 tsp. PEPPER
1/4 cup DRY BREAD CRUMBS
1 Tbsp. BUTTER, melted

Cut broccoli into florets. Peel stalks and cut into 1/4-inch thick rounds. Put stalk slices in the bottom of a steamer basket in a large saucepan filled with about 1/2 inch of water. Add florets on top. Cover and steam over medium-high heat for 7-10 minutes or until just tender. In a bowl, combine eggs, cottage cheese, cheddar cheese, onion, Worcestershire sauce, salt and pepper and mix well. Arrange broccoli in a shallow 1 1/2-quart baking dish and cover with cheese mixture. In a small bowl, combine bread crumbs and butter and toss; sprinkle on top of casserole. Bake, uncovered, at 350° for 15-20 minutes or until heated through and egg mixture is set. Serve immediately.

Camp Pendleton

In 1942, the 250,000-acre Rancho Santa Margarita y Los Flores became Marine Corps Base Camp Joseph H. Pendleton, the nation's busiest military base. Over 60,000 military and civilian personnel work aboard the base every day. The original Ranch House, Museum and Chapel, built in the mid-1800s, are listed as a National Historic Site as well as a California State Historical Landmark.

Red Bliss Potato Boats

Jeffrey Starr—Culinary Director and Winery Chef, Sutter Home
Family Vineyards, St. Helena

12 RED BLISS POTATOES (baby red potatoes)
OLIVE OIL, as needed
SALT and PEPPER to taste
1 lb. GOAT CHEESE, crumbled
1/4 cup toasted PINE NUTS
1/4 cup oil-packed SUN-DRIED TOMATOES, drained, patted dry
   and chopped
1/4 cup chopped KALAMATA OLIVES
2 Tbsp. snipped fresh CHIVES
2 Tbsp. chopped fresh ITALIAN PARSLEY

Toss the potatoes in enough olive oil to coat; season with salt
and pepper and roast in a 350° oven 20-30 minutes. Remove
from oven and let cool just enough to handle. Cut potatoes in
half. With a small spoon, scoop out about 1 teaspoon of the
potato to create a small potato "boat." Fill each potato with
about 1 tablespoon of goat cheese, a sprinkling of pine nuts,
tomatoes and olives. Transfer the potatoes to a platter and
sprinkle with chives and parsley. Serve warm.

Aunt Joan's Zucchini

Mariquita Farms—Watsonville

2 Tbsp. OLIVE OIL
3 cloves GARLIC, minced
1 1/2 lbs. thinly sliced SUMMER SQUASH (your preference)
SALT and PEPPER to taste
1/4 tsp. chopped fresh BASIL
1/4 cup grated PARMESAN CHEESE

In a skillet, heat oil over moderate heat; add garlic and cook
for just a few seconds *(do not brown)*. Stir in squash and cook
until lightly browned on the bottom. Continue stirring and
cooking until all squash is lightly browned, adding oil as
needed. Season with salt and pepper. Remove squash mixture
to a serving dish and top with basil and Parmesan.

Brussels Sprouts with Tangy Dijon Vinaigrette

Brussels sprouts have never tasted so good! With its clean, sharp flavor, Dijon mustard adds a pleasant bite to this rich, mahogany-colored chilled dressing.

Capurro Marketing, LLC—Moss Landing

1 pkg. (12 oz.) TOPLESS VEG QUICKIES™ BRUSSELS SPROUTS
1 Tbsp. OLIVE OIL
Pinch of SALT

Tangy Dijon Vinaigrette:
  3 Tbsp. DIJON MUSTARD
  1/3 cup RED WINE VINEGAR
  3/4 cup OLIVE OIL
  SALT and PEPPER to taste
  2 tsp. fresh DILL
  1/2 lb. MUSHROOMS, sliced
  1 RED BELL PEPPER, julienned and cut into 1-inch strips

1 head BUTTER LETTUCE
1 head RED LEAF LETTUCE
Freshly grated PARMESAN CHEESE

In a saucepan, bring oil, salt and enough water to cover sprouts to a boil. Wash and trim sprouts and add to boiling water; parboil for approximately 5 minutes, until just tender. Drain. In a large mixing bowl, blend together mustard, vinegar, oil, salt, pepper and dill. Add Brussels sprouts, mushrooms and bell pepper to vinaigrette; toss well to coat vegetables. Place in refrigerator and marinate for at least 1 hour. To serve, line a platter or individual serving plates with both types of lettuce leaves. Spoon marinated vegetable mixture onto lettuce and garnish with Parmesan.

From Brussels With Love

Brussels sprouts were initially cultivated in Italy, and then near Brussels, Belgium. Today the majority of the United States supply comes from California's central coast.

Mascarpone Polenta with Onion & Portobello Ragout

Paul Hatfield, Corporate Chef—Mozzarella Fresca Inc., Benicia

2 Tbsp. BUTTER
1/2 cup finely chopped ONION
2 cups CHICKEN STOCK
1 cup MILK
SALT and freshly ground PEPPER to taste
1 cup YELLOW CORNMEAL
1/2 cup MASCARPONE CHEESE

In a saucepan, melt butter and sauté onion until translucent. Add chicken stock and milk and bring to a boil. Season with salt and pepper. Gradually and steadily pour cornmeal into saucepan, stirring constantly with a wooden spoon. Continue to stir and cook until mixture pulls away from the side of the pan, about 20 minutes. Adjust consistency with water, stock or milk as needed to prevent mixture from thickening too much. Remove from heat and add mascarpone about 5 minutes prior to serving. Serve topped with **Portobello Ragout** and garnished with a rosemary sprig.

Portobello Ragout

2 Tbsp. BUTTER
3 PORTOBELLO CAPS, sliced
1 lg. ONION, sliced
2 Tbsp. TOMATO PASTE
2 tsp. minced fresh ROSEMARY
1/2 cup CHICKEN STOCK
SALT and freshly ground PEPPER to taste

In a saucepan, melt butter and sauté mushrooms and onion for about 15 minutes. Stir in tomato paste and rosemary; sauté 5 minutes more. Add chicken stock and adjust seasoning. Reduce until liquid evaporates and sauce thickens.

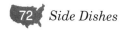

Breads

Avocado Bread

Nancy Adams—Indian Wells

2 EGGS
3/4 cup SUGAR
1/2 cup SALAD OIL
1 tsp. VANILLA
1 cup mashed CALIFORNIA AVOCADOS
1 1/2 cups FLOUR, sifted
1 tsp. BAKING POWDER
1 tsp. SALT
1 tsp. CINNAMON
3/4 tsp. ALLSPICE
1 cup chopped, roasted PECANS (optional)

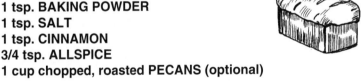

In a mixing bowl, beat eggs until fluffy. Add sugar, oil and vanilla and mix until well-blended. Stir in avocados. In a separate bowl, combine flour, baking powder, salt, cinnamon and allspice and mix well. Add flour mixture to creamed mixture; fold in pecans. Pour batter into two 8 x 4 loaf pans sprayed with cooking spray. Bake at 350° for 45-50 minutes or until a toothpick inserted in center comes out clean.

Mandarin Orange Pumpkin Bread

Sunkist Growers, Inc.—Sherman Oaks

1 SUNKIST® MANDARIN ORANGE
2/3 cup BUTTER
2 2/3 cups SUGAR
4 EGGS
1 can (16 oz.) PUMPKIN
2/3 cup fresh-squeezed JUICE of a
   SUNKIST® MANDARIN ORANGE

3 1/3 cups ALL-PURPOSE
   FLOUR
2 tsp. BAKING SODA
1 1/2 tsp. SALT
1/2 tsp. BAKING POWDER
2 tsp. PUMPKIN PIE SPICE
2/3 cup chopped PECANS

Preheat oven to 350°. Butter or spray non-stick coating on bottoms of two 9-inch loaf pans. Remove peel from orange using a grater or zesting tool, being careful not to remove the white pith. Cut off pith and chop mandarin, removing any tough membranes. Set aside peel and pulp. In a mixer, cream butter and sugar together, and add eggs one at a time, mixing until smooth. Add pumpkin, mandarin juice and reserved peel and pulp. In a separate bowl, mix together flour, baking soda, salt, baking powder and pumpkin pie spice. Slowly add dry ingredients to pumpkin mixture and mix until blended. Stir in nuts and then pour into loaf pans. Bake 1 hour and 10 minutes or until a toothpick inserted in center comes out clean. Let cool completely before removing from pan.

California's Missions

Stretching from San Diego to Sonoma, just north of San Francisco, California's El Camino Real (Spanish for "The Royal Road"), links 21 Spanish missions. The first mission, San Diego de Alcalá, was established in 1769 by Father Junípero Serra; the last, some 600 miles northward, San Francisco Solano, was built in 1823. All of these missions have been restored to some extent.

Blue Cornmeal Bread

Barbara Costa—Dunbar House, 1880, Murphys

2 1/4 cups ALL-PURPOSE
　FLOUR
1 3/4 cups BLUE CORNMEAL
1 cup SUGAR
1/3 cup toasted PINE NUTS
3/4 tsp. BAKING POWDER
3/4 tsp. BAKING SODA

3/4 tsp. SALT
1 1/4 cups WHOLE MILK
3/4 cup VEGETABLE OIL
3 EGGS
1/2 cup BUTTERMILK
1 1/2 cups frozen CORN,
　thawed and drained

Preheat oven to 350°. Butter a 13 x 9 glass baking dish. In a mixing bowl, whisk together flour, cornmeal, sugar, pine nuts, baking powder, baking soda and salt until blended. In a separate bowl, whisk together milk, oil, eggs and buttermilk. Add wet mixture to dry ingredients and whisk until just blended. Fold in corn. Pour batter into baking dish. Bake for about 40 minutes, until a toothpick inserted in the center comes out clean. Cut into 2-inch squares and serve warm.

Berry-Walnut Muffins

Diamond of California—Stockton

2 cups FLOUR
1 1/2 tsp. BAKING POWDER
1 tsp. BAKING SODA
1/2 tsp. SALT
3/4 cup BUTTERMILK
3/4 cup packed LIGHT
　BROWN SUGAR

1/2 cup UNSALTED BUTTER,
　melted
2 EGGS
1 tsp. VANILLA
1 cup fresh BERRIES*
1/2 cup + 2 Tbsp. DIAMOND®
　SLICED WALNUTS, toasted

Preheat oven to 350°. Line 14-16 muffin cups with paper liners. In a large bowl, whisk together flour, baking powder, baking soda and salt. In a separate bowl, whisk together buttermilk, brown sugar, butter, eggs and vanilla. Stir berries and 1/2 cup walnuts into buttermilk mixture and then stir in dry ingredients until just moistened. Fill muffin cups 3/4 full and sprinkle with remaining walnuts. Bake 20-25 minutes or until a toothpick inserted in the center comes out clean. Cool for 5 minutes in pan and transfer to a wire rack.

*Fresh or unsweetened frozen raspberries, blackberries or blueberries.

Grandma Urkey's Scotch Scones

"Grandma Urkey (Essie Urquhart), who was Scottish, crossed the country by wagon to California in the 1870s. This is her traditional Scottish scone recipe—very simple and very good."

Pam Service—Clarke Historical Museum, Eureka

2 cups FLOUR	2 Tbsp. SUGAR
4 tsp. BAKING POWDER	1 cup MILK
1/2 tsp. SALT	

In a mixing bowl, combine all ingredients and mix to form a rather wet dough. Place dough on a generously floured surface and sprinkle with additional flour. With a floured rolling pin, roll out dough to 1/2-inch thickness and cut into irregular shapes. Place on an ungreased cookie sheet. Bake at 250° for 35 minutes; *do not brown*. Scones should be nearly white when done. Split, toast and serve with butter and jam.

Indian Fry Bread

"Living near Bishop, we were close to the Paiute Indian Tribe. During our Tri-County Fair, their fry bread stand was the busiest concession of all. My family makes this bread as a base for a variety of tacos."

Carol Dillon—Grandma's Custom Baskets, Fresno

3 cups FLOUR	3 (level) Tbsp. LARD
3 tsp. BAKING POWDER	About 1 1/2 cups LUKEWARM
3 tsp. SALT	WATER

In a bowl, combine flour, baking powder and salt and mix well. Using fingertips, blend in lard until mixture is crumbly. Add enough lukewarm water to make a stiff dough; knead for 2-3 minutes. On a lightly floured surface, roll a thin dough out; pat or cut into circles. Deep fry in 400° oil about 1 1/2 minutes per side, until puffed and golden brown.

Panettone

(Italian Christmas Bread)

"This is a modified version of the panettone my mother, of Italian descent, used to make. Dried fruit has been substituted for candied fruit."

Jan Brosseau—Inn at the Pinnacles, Soledad

1 Tbsp. DRY YEAST	1 Tbsp. grated LEMON PEEL
1/3 cup SUGAR	1 tsp. SALT
1/2 cup WARM WATER (110°)	1/4 cup chopped PECANS
4 cups FLOUR	1/4 cup chopped MIXED
4 EGGS, beaten	DRIED FRUIT
1/2 cup lukewarm melted BUTTER	1/2 cup DARK RAISINS
1 tsp. VANILLA	1/2 cup GOLDEN RAISINS

In a bowl, dissolve yeast and sugar in warm water. Add 1 cup of the flour and beat for about 2 minutes. Add eggs, butter, vanilla, lemon peel, salt and remaining flour and mix to form dough. Knead dough for about 5 minutes and place in a bowl. Cover lightly and let rise in a warm place for 1 hour or until finger indentation remains. Knead in pecans, dried fruit and raisins. Spread dough in a greased panettone pan or two 7-inch round cake pans. Let rise in a warm place for 1 hour. Bake at 350° for 40-50 minutes or until panettone tests done. Let cool in pan for 15 minutes; remove and cool thoroughly on wire rack.

What is a Sea Otter?

A sea otter is a marine mammal that lives in California's coastal waters. To eat, they dive up to 120 feet to find clams, crabs, snails, starfish, abalone and other marine animals. They then surface, lie on their backs and use their stomachs as a table. Sometimes they use tools, such as a rock, to help them open hard-shelled prey. Sea otters usually swim on their backs at the water's surface using their rear flippers to move and their tails to steer.

Tomato Rosemary Focaccia

This flavorful focaccia is great with pasta dishes or with a bowl of tomato soup. It's worth the effort!

California Tomato Commission—Fresno

1 pkg. (.25 oz.) DRY YEAST
2 cups WARM WATER (110-115°)
1/2 cup OLIVE OIL
3 Tbsp. BUTTER, softened
1/2 cup MILK
1 Tbsp. minced fresh ROSEMARY
3 3/4-4 cups ALL-PURPOSE FLOUR
1 tsp. SALT
SEMOLINA FLOUR or CORNMEAL, as needed
4 CALIFORNIA ROMA TOMATOES, sliced 1/8-inch thick
1 Tbsp. ROSEMARY LEAVES
1/2 tsp. SALT or KOSHER SALT

Preheat oven to 425°. In a small bowl, dissolve yeast in warm water; let stand for 5-10 minutes until foamy. In a mixing bowl, combine yeast, 2 tablespoons of olive oil, butter, milk and rosemary. Slowly add flour while mixing on low speed; continue adding flour until a soft dough forms, adding only enough flour to make dough manageable. Knead dough until smooth, 5-10 minutes. Place in a bowl and cover with a towel; let rise in warm place for 1-2 hours or until doubled in bulk. Punch down dough and divide into 6 equal pieces. Shape each piece into a flattened 5-inch round, cover with a towel and let rest for 10-15 minutes. Place rounds on a baking sheet lightly sprinkled with semolina flour. Using fingertips, poke many small holes in each. Recover rounds with a towel and let rise in a warm place for 1 hour or until doubled in size. Poke each round again with fingertips. Arrange tomato slices in a circle on top. Drizzle with 1/4 cup of olive oil and sprinkle with rosemary leaves and salt. Bake at 425° for 20-30 minutes or until golden brown. Brush with remaining 2 tablespoons olive oil; remove from baking sheet and cool on wire racks.

Prune Cake

"This is my French grandmother's recipe. She passed the recipe down to my mother."

James W. Lenhoff—Butte County Historical Society, Oroville

1/2 cup SHORTENING	1/2 tsp. NUTMEG
1 1/2 cups SUGAR	1/2 tsp. ALLSPICE
3 EGGS, well-beaten	1 cup SOUR MILK or
2 1/4 cups FLOUR	BUTTERMILK
1/2 tsp. SALT	1 cup chopped or mashed
1 tsp. BAKING SODA	stewed fresh PRUNES
1 tsp. BAKING POWDER	WHIPPED CREAM
1/2 tsp. CINNAMON	

In a bowl, cream together shortening and sugar until fluffy; blend in eggs. In a separate bowl, sift together flour, salt, baking soda, baking powder and spices. Add to creamed mixture alternately with the sour milk. Blend in prunes. Pour batter into 2 greased (9-inch) cake pans. Bake at 350° for 30-40 minutes or until a toothpick inserted in the center comes out clean. Remove from pans and let cool on wire racks. Spread whipped cream between layers, on sides and top. Refrigerate for at least 30 minutes.

"California's Gold" Peach Cobbler

"This California dessert recipe has been in our family for over 40 years. It belonged to my mother, noted San Joaquin Valley Mexican dessert cookbook author, Socorro Muñoz Kimble. She emigrated to California from Mexico in the 1930s. Peaches are one of California's top agricultural products. We produce them in Kern County and export them around the world!

Lisa Edmonston—Bakersfield

1 EGG	2 Tbsp. + 1 cup SUGAR
1/2 tsp. VANILLA	6 Tbsp. BUTTER
1 cup FLOUR	3 cups sliced fresh PEACHES
1 tsp. BAKING POWDER	2 tsp. CINNAMON

Preheat oven to 425°. In a bowl, beat together egg and vanilla. In a separate bowl, sift together flour, baking powder and 2 tablespoons of sugar. Cut in 3 tablespoons of butter until mixture is crumbly. Add egg mixture and stir well. Spoon batter into a greased 13 x 9 baking dish. Arrange peaches on top. In a small bowl, combine cinnamon and remaining sugar and mix well; sprinkle mixture on top of peaches. Melt remaining butter and drizzle over cobbler. Bake, uncovered, for 30-35 minutes.

Sacramento–California's Capital City

In 1839, John A. Sutter established a colony and fort just east of the Sacramento River on a 50,000-acre Mexican land grant. His fort became the western terminal for early pioneers. In 1848, gold was discovered at one of his saw-mills and the Gold Rush of 1849 began. His son, John A. Sutter Jr., founded the town of Sacramento. Incorporated as a city in 1850, it became the state capital in 1854. Today, it is the commer-cial center of a rich farming region and, due to a deep-water channel to San Francisco Bay, has become a major inland port.

Fresh Fig Dessert Pizza

California Fresh Fig Growers Association—Fresno

1 roll (18 oz.) refrigerated SUGAR COOKIE DOUGH
4 oz. CREAM CHEESE, softened
1/4 cup MASCARPONE CHEESE or SOUR CREAM
1 EGG
8 lg. (1 lb.) CALIFORNIA FIGS, quartered
1/4 cup CURRANT or APPLE JELLY
2 tsp. fresh LEMON JUICE

Preheat oven to 325°. Slice cookie dough and place in a single layer on a 12-inch pizza pan. Allow to stand a few minutes at room temperature until softened. Flour hands generously and press dough together evenly to about 1/4-inch thick, leaving a 1/2-inch raised edge. Bake for 10 minutes or until lightly browned. Cool. In a small bowl, combine cream cheese, mascarpone and egg. Beat until smooth. Spread evenly over crust, avoiding edges. Bake 15-20 minutes or until filling is set and lightly browned. Cool. Just before serving, arrange fig slices on top. In a saucepan, over low heat, melt jelly and stir in lemon juice; brush onto figs.

By Any Other Name?

"The Golden State" became California's official state nick-name in 1968. It is also known as "The Land of Milk and Honey," "The El Dorado State," and "The Grape State."

Date Sunflower Cookies

Judy Higgins—Shields Date Gardens, Indio

1/2 cup CINNAMON APPLESAUCE
1/2 cup BUTTER, melted
2 1/2 cups FLOUR
1 cup SUGAR
1/2 cup MOLASSES
2 EGGS
1 tsp. VANILLA
1/2 tsp. BAKING SODA
2 cups chopped DATES
1 cup UNSALTED
    SUNFLOWER SEEDS

In a bowl, combine all the ingredients and mix well. Drop by teaspoonfuls onto a greased baking sheet. Bake at 375° for 9 minutes or until golden.

Avocado Cheesecake

California Avocado Commission—Santa Ana

2 cups GRAHAM CRACKER CRUMBS
1 1/3 cups ground PINE NUTS
1/2 cup melted BUTTER
4 CALIFORNIA AVOCADOS, peeled and mashed
2 cartons (8 oz. ea.) CREAM CHEESE, softened
1 cup SUGAR
6 EGGS
1 Tbsp. grated LIME PEEL
1/4 cup LIME JUICE, freshly squeezed
2 tsp. VANILLA
1/3 cup HEAVY CREAM, whipped to soft peaks

Topping:
   3 cups SOUR CREAM
   2 Tbsp. SUGAR
   1 tsp. VANILLA

1/2 cup PINE NUTS

Preheat oven to 350°. In a medium bowl, place graham cracker crumbs, pine nuts and butter; toss to mix well. Press graham cracker mixture on bottom and sides of a 9-inch springform pan to make the crust. In a large mixing bowl, combine avocados, cream cheese and sugar. Cream ingredients together well. While mixing constantly, add eggs one at a time. Add lime peel, lime juice and vanilla; mix. Fold in whipped cream. Pour batter into the springform pan and bake for 30 minutes or until center is set. Remove cheesecake from oven (leaving the oven on) and let cool for 10 minutes. In a small bowl, stir together topping ingredients. Spread topping on cheesecake and sprinkle with pine nuts. Return cheesecake to oven and bake for 5 more minutes. Remove from oven and refrigerate 6-8 hours, until thoroughly chilled and firm.

California Avocados

California is the number one producer of avocados in the U.S. Most California avocados are harvested on 60,000 acres between San Luis Obispo and the Mexican border.

 *Desserts*

Strawberry Shortcake

California Strawberry Commission—Watsonville

2 pints CALIFORNIA STRAWBERRIES
1 Tbsp. SUGAR

Biscuits:
    2 cups ALL-PURPOSE FLOUR   1/4 cup BUTTER
    3 Tbsp. SUGAR   1/4 cup SHORTENING
    4 tsp. BAKING POWDER   2/3 cup SOUR CREAM
    Dash of SALT

1 EGG WHITE, beaten
SUGAR
1 cup WHIPPING CREAM
1 Tbsp. SUGAR

Rinse and hull strawberries; pat dry. Place strawberries in a bowl, sprinkle with sugar and set aside. To make biscuits: In a bowl, sift flour and combine with other dry ingredients. Cut in butter and shortening until mixture resembles coarse crumbs. Lightly mix in sour cream. Divide dough into 6 equal portions. On a lightly floured board, pat each portion into a 3-inch circle; place on a greased baking sheet and brush with egg white. Sprinkle tops generously with additional sugar. Bake in a 415° oven for 15 minutes or until golden brown. Remove from oven and cool on a rack. In a bowl, combine whipping cream with sugar and beat until soft peaks form. Slice each shortcake in half horizontally. Fill with strawberries and top with whipped cream. Garnish with additional strawberries.

Yosemite National Park

Set aside as a national park in 1890, Yosemite embraces a spectacular tract of mountain and valley scenery. Highlights include Yosemite Valley and its high cliffs and waterfalls; Wawona's History Center and historic hotel; Mariposa Grove, which contains hundreds of ancient giant sequoias; Glacier Point's spectacular views; Tuolumne Meadows and Hetch Hetchy Reservoir.

Chocolate Soufflé

Chef John Ash in association with Fetzer Vineyards—San Rafael

BUTTER and SUGAR
8 oz. BITTERSWEET CHOCOLATE,
  coarsely chopped
1 Tbsp. UNSALTED BUTTER
1 Tbsp. ALL-PURPOSE FLOUR
1/3 cup MILK
1 tsp. VANILLA
4 EGGS, separated

2 tsp. grated ORANGE PEEL
1/4 tsp. CREAM OF TARTAR
Pinch of KOSHER SALT
1/4 cup SUGAR
POWDERED SUGAR to taste
Strained, lightly sweetened
  RASPBERRY PURÉE

Preheat oven to 375°. Lightly butter soufflé dishe(es)* and sprinkle with granulated sugar. Place chocolate in a double boiler and melt, stirring occasionally. In a separate saucepan, melt the butter, add flour and cook over low heat for 3 minutes. Add milk and whisk until mixture is smooth and lightly thickened. Cook for 5 minutes until mixture thickens. Remove from heat, whisk in melted chocolate, vanilla, egg yolks and orange peel. Transfer to a large bowl and set aside. In a separate bowl, beat egg whites with cream of tartar and salt until soft peaks form. Sprinkle in 1/4 cup sugar gradually and continue to beat until whites are stiff but not dry. Stir 1/4 of whites into the chocolate mixture to lighten it. Carefully fold in remaining whites. Pour mixture into prepared soufflé dish(es) and set on a baking sheet. (The soufflé can be prepared to this point and refrigerated overnight.) Bake for 35-40 minutes (15-17 minutes for the individual soufflés) or until a toothpick inserted in the center comes out moist but not wet. Remove from oven, dust with powdered sugar and serve immediately with raspberry purée.

*Makes 1 (1 1/2 qt.) soufflé or 8 (1/2 cup) individual soufflés. Increase baking time slightly if refrigerated.

Suggested wine: Fetzer® Reserve Port

California Grapes
More than 300,000 tons of grapes are grown in California annually.

Strawberry-Apple Cobbler

This non fat signature dish is like a torte. It tastes fabulous!

Mäni's Bakery & Cafe—Los Angeles

1 cup APPLE JUICE (not from concentrate)
1 Tbsp. LEMON JUICE
1/2 tsp. CINNAMON
2 Tbsp. FLOUR
6 cups peeled and sliced TART APPLES
3 cups STRAWBERRIES
3 EGG WHITES
1/2 cup frozen APPLE JUICE CONCENTRATE, thawed
1 cup WHOLE-WHEAT PASTRY FLOUR
1/3 cup NON FAT DRY MILK
1/3 cup ROLLED OATS

Preheat oven to 425°. In a small bowl, whisk together apple and lemon juices, cinnamon and flour. Place apples in a 11 x 9 baking dish. Pour juice mixture over the apples and bake for 25 minutes. Reduce oven temperature to 350° and continue baking. When apples are tender, stir in strawberries. In a bowl, whip egg whites until soft peaks form. Add apple juice concentrate and whip until stiff peaks form. In a separate bowl, mix together the pastry flour, dry milk and oats; gently fold into egg whites *(do not overmix)*. Drop the batter by large spoonfuls over fruit and bake an additional 25 minutes or until browned.

Sequoia & Kings Canyon National Parks

The Generals Highway climbs over 5,000 feet to the awe-inspiring sequoia groves. From there, trails lead to the high alpine wilderness which makes up most of the park. Beneath the park's surface lie over 200 caverns.

Top 5 giant sequoias:

Name	Height	Girth	
General Sherman	274.9	102.6	*These giants are esti-*
Washington	254.7	101.1	*mated to range in age*
General Grant	268.1	107.5	*from 1,800 to 2,700*
President	240.9	93.0	*years old.*
Lincoln	255.8	98.3	

Pear & Raisin Cobbler with Cheddar Topping

California Pear Advisory Board—Sacramento

6 lg. slightly under-ripe **CALIFORNIA BARTLETT PEARS,**
    peeled, cored and sliced
1/2 cup **RAISINS**
1/2 cup **SUGAR**
1 Tbsp. **WATER**
1 Tbsp. + 1 tsp. **CORNSTARCH**
1 Tbsp. **LEMON JUICE**
1/2 tsp. **CINNAMON**

Preheat oven to 400°. Butter a 2-quart shallow baking dish and set aside. In a saucepan, combine all ingredients. Cook over medium heat until pears are hot and mixture is slightly thick, about 5 minutes; pour into baking dish. Drop *Cheddar Cheese Topping* by teaspoonfuls over pear filling. Bake for 25-30 minutes or until topping is set, tenting the dish loosely with foil if topping browns too quickly. Let cool slightly and serve.

Cheddar Cheese Topping

1 1/2 cups **FLOUR**
1/2 cup **SUGAR**
2 1/2 tsp. **BAKING POWDER**
3 tsp. **BUTTER,** softened

2/3 cup finely shredded
    SHARP CHEDDAR CHEESE
4 tsp. **MILK**
1 **EGG**

In a bowl, stir together dry ingredients. Cut in butter with a pastry blender or fork until mixture resembles coarse crumbs. Stir in cheese, milk and egg (mixture will be very thick).

California State Railroad Museum

In Sacramento, visit this museum—the largest of its kind in North America—to see 21 restored locomotives and train cars, exhibits, dioramas, pictures and murals that document the history of American railroading.

Plum-Good Peanutter Bars

California Dried Plum Board—Sacramento

1 cup packed BROWN SUGAR
1/2 cup CRUNCHY PEANUT BUTTER
2 Tbsp. BUTTER or MARGARINE, softened
1/2 cup FAT FREE MILK
1 EGG
1 tsp. VANILLA
1 cup OLD-FASHIONED or QUICK OATS
1 1/2 cups ALL-PURPOSE FLOUR
1 tsp. BAKING POWDER
1/2 tsp. SALT
1 cup coarsely chopped DRIED PLUMS
POWDERED SUGAR (optional)

Preheat oven to 350°. Lightly spray a 13 x 9 baking pan with nonstick cooking spray. In a mixing bowl, beat together sugar, peanut butter and butter on medium speed until creamy. Add milk, egg and vanilla; beat well. In a separate bowl, combine oats, flour, baking powder and salt; add to peanut butter mixture, mixing on low speed until well-blended. Stir in dried plums. Press batter evenly into baking pan and bake 25-30 minutes or until golden brown. Cool in pan on wire rack. Sprinkle with powdered sugar.

A Prune by Any Other Name!

All prunes are plums, but not all plums are prunes. Dried plum varieties can be dried without fermenting while still containing the pits. Today, there are more than 80,000 high production acres concentrated in the Sacramento, Santa Clara, Sonoma, Napa and San Joaquin Valleys of California. Currently, these acres produce more than twice as many dried plums as the rest of the world combined— approximately 99 percent of the American supply and 70 percent of the world supply.

Guiltless California Cheesecake

Real California Cheese—Modesto

*Note: Make the **Non Fat Yogurt Cheese** at least 12 hours before starting this recipe.*

1 cup LOW FAT GRAHAM CRACKER CRUMBS
2 Tbsp. BUTTER, melted
1 1/2 cups SUGAR
3 EGGS
1/4 cup FLOUR
1 Tbsp. VANILLA
1 tsp. grated LEMON PEEL

Preheat oven to 350°. In a bowl, toss together cracker crumbs and butter. Pat evenly over bottom of a 9-inch springform pan. Bake 10 minutes or until golden. Remove from oven and set aside. Raise oven temperature to 450°. In a mixing bowl, beat 6 cups *Non Fat Yogurt Cheese,* sugar and eggs on high speed for 1 minute. Mix in flour, vanilla and lemon peel until just blended. Pour into prepared crust and bake for 10 minutes. Reduce oven temperature to 250° and continue to bake for 1 hour or until center is set. Run a thin-bladed knife between cake and pan. Cool slightly and then refrigerate, uncovered, until cake is completely chilled (at least 3 hours). Garnish with assorted berries and/or sliced fruit as desired.

Non Fat Yogurt Cheese

4 qts. NON FAT PLAIN YOGURT (no gelatin)

Set a colander over a large bowl, supporting the colander so the base is at least 2 inches above the bottom of the bowl. Line colander with 2 layers of cheesecloth. Spoon in yogurt and cover tightly with plastic wrap. Refrigerate and let drain for 12 hours. (When done, yogurt cheese should have the soft yet firm consistency of cream cheese.)

Note: The longer you strain the yogurt, the drier it will become and the more it will resemble cream cheese.

Almond Cake with Caramelized Apricots

Chef Andy Powning—GreenLeaf Produce, San Francisco

7 oz. BUTTER, softened
12 oz. ALMOND PASTE
3/4 cup SUGAR
5 EGGS, room temperature
Grated PEEL of 1 ORANGE
1/2 tsp VANILLA

1/2 tsp ALMOND EXTRACT
1/2 cup FLOUR
1 tsp. BAKING POWDER
1/4 tsp. SALT
WHIPPED CREAM

Using an electric mixer, cream together butter, almond paste and sugar. Continue mixing, adding eggs one at a time. Blend in orange peel and flavorings. Sift together dry ingredients and stir into creamed mixture. Arrange **Caramelized Apricots** in bottom of a cake pan; pour remaining caramel over top. Pour cake batter over apricots. Place pan on a cookie sheet lined with parchment and bake at 325° for about 30 minutes. Cake will brown and spring back to the touch when done. Remove from oven. Let cake cool for five minutes and then carefully invert onto serving plate. Serve with whipped cream.

Caramelized Apricots

1 cup SUGAR
12 firm APRICOTS, halved

In a heavy-bottomed skillet, caramelize sugar to a deep golden brown. Add apricots; turn to coat and cook briefly, until browned but still apricot-shaped. Remove from heat.

Lake Tahoe

This beautiful glacial lake lies in a valley of the Sierra Nevada on the California-Nevada border. The lake is 23 miles long, 12 miles wide and 1,640 feet deep at its deepest point, making it one of the deepest lakes in the continental U.S. For a magnificent view of Lake Tahoe and the Sierra Nevada range, take the ski lift to the top of Heavenly Mountain.

Julia's Perfect Pumpkin Pie

"This recipe makes the best pumpkin pie we have ever eaten."

Julia Wiley—Mariquita Farms, Watsonville

1 med. SUGAR PIE PUMPKIN

Pie Crust:

1 1/4 cups FLOUR
1/2 tsp. SALT
2 tsp. SUGAR
4 Tbsp. cold SHORTENING

4 Tbsp. cold UNSALTED
   BUTTER
3-6 Tbsp. ICE COLD WATER

Pumpkin Pie Filling:

1 tsp. GINGER
2 tsp. CINNAMON
1/2 tsp. CLOVES
1/2 tsp. NUTMEG

1/2 tsp. SALT
1 cup packed BROWN SUGAR
4 EGGS
1 1/3 cups HALF and HALF

Preheat oven to 350°. Cut pumpkin in 1/2; discard seeds. Place pumpkin cut-side down in a glass baking dish. Bake for 45-60 minutes, until a fork easily pierces the entire wall of the pumpkin. Remove from oven; let cool. To make crust: In a food processor, combine flour, salt and sugar and mix well. Add chunked shortening and butter to processor and pulse 3-5 times until mixture is crumbly; place in a mixing bowl and combine with 3 tablespoons of cold water. Add additional water 1/2 tablespoon at a time, mixing with hands, until dough is soft and easy to handle. Pat into a thick disk; wrap in waxed paper and refrigerate for 30 minutes. Roll dough out on a lightly floured surface to a 13-inch circle. Place in a 10-inch pie plate and trim to 1/2 inch beyond the edge; flute edges. Place aluminum foil or parchment paper on top of crust; add pie weights or dried beans. Bake at 350° for 10 minutes. To make filling: Scoop pulp from pumpkin; place in food processor and purée. Pour 2 cups of purée into a saucepan. Stir spices and brown sugar into purée and bring to a soft boil. In a food processor, combine eggs with half and half and blend; add to the pumpkin mixture. Cook for 2-3 minutes, stirring occasionally. Pour filling into crust and bake for 25 minutes or until center is still slightly wobbly. Cool on a wire rack for at least 1 hour.

Strawberry Pizza

"This is a great summer dessert!"

Carol Dillon—Grandma's Custom Baskets, Fresno

2 pints STRAWBERRIES, sliced
1 1/4 cups SUGAR
1/4 cup WATER
1 roll (18 oz.) refrigerated SUGAR
   COOKIE DOUGH
1 pkg. (8 oz.) CREAM CHEESE

2 EGGS
2 Tbsp. LEMON JUICE,
   divided
2 Tbsp. CORNSTARCH
WHIPPED CREAM

In a bowl, combine strawberries, 1/2 cup sugar and water. Refrigerate for at least 2 hours; drain and reserve juice. Slice cookie dough and place on a lightly greased pizza pan; press edges together to form the crust. Bake at 350° for 10 minutes or until lightly browned; set aside. In a mixing bowl, beat together softened cream cheese and 1/2 cup sugar until fluffy. Add eggs, one at a time, mixing lightly after each addition; beat in 1 tablespoon lemon juice. Spread mixture over hot crust. Bake for 10-12 minutes. In a saucepan, combine cornstarch and 1/4 cup sugar. Add reserved strawberry juice and stir until blended; add lemon juice. Bring mixture to a boil and cook for several minutes until liquid is clear and mixture has thickened; let cool. Pour mixture over strawberries, stirring gently to combine, and then spread evenly over filling. Top with whipped cream.

Death Valley National Park

Death Valley was proclaimed a national monument in 1933 and a national park in 1994. Death Valley National Park comprises more than 3.3 million acres, including more than 3 million acres of wilderness. It is the largest national park outside of Alaska. The name is foreboding and gloomy, yet here in this valley—much of it below sea level—or in its surrounding mountains, you can find spectacular wildflower displays, snow covered peaks, beautiful sand dunes, abandoned mines and the hottest place in North America!

Baked Apples
with Orange Sauce

"This is one of the most requested desserts at our Inn."

Debra La Rochelle—Sutter Creek Inn, Sutter Creek

4 FUJI or GRANNY SMITH APPLES, cored

Filling:
- 2 Tbsp. RAISINS
- 2 Tbsp. chopped WALNUTS
- 1/4 cup packed BROWN SUGAR
- 1 tsp. CINNAMON

Orange Sauce:
- 2 Tbsp. LIGHT CORN SYRUP
- 1 Tbsp. packed LIGHT BROWN SUGAR
- 1 Tbsp. BUTTER
- 4 Tbsp. WATER
- 6 Tbsp. HEAVY WHIPPING CREAM
- 1/2 tsp. ORANGE LIQUEUR
- JUICE and grated PEEL from 1 ORANGE

In a bowl, combine all the filling ingredients and mix well. Stuff apples with filling and place in a baking pan. Bake at 350° for 30-45 minutes, until tender. To make orange sauce: In a heavy saucepan, combine syrup, brown sugar and butter. Cook over low heat for several minutes, until butter has melted and mixture has thickened. Add water and boil for 3 minutes. Stir in cream and liqueur and continue to boil for 1 more minute. Reduce heat; stir in orange juice and peel. Pour over apples.

Palm Springs

With its almost 350 days of sunshine per year, an average daily temperature of 75° and more than 100 golf courses, it is easy to see why this has become one of California's favorite resort cities. An aerial tramway based at nearby Chino Canyon transports passengers 2.5 miles (with vertical ascent of 5,873 feet) up to the east edge of Long Valley. The tram affords spectacular views of the rugged San Jacinto Mountains.

Cuccidati

(Italian Fig Cookies)

"Making these cookies is a Sicilian holiday tradition handed down from my father's side of the family."

Jan Brosseau—Inn at the Pinnacles, Soledad

Dough:
- 1 1/2 cups SUGAR
- 1 lb. MARGARINE
- 1 tsp. VANILLA
- 4 EGGS
- 7 cups ALL-PURPOSE FLOUR
- 7 tsp. BAKING POWDER

Filling:
- 3 pkgs. (6-10 oz. ea.) DRIED FIGS (white, black or mixed)
- 1 box (15 oz.) DARK RAISINS
- 1 pkg. (12 oz.) pitted DATES
- 1 pkg. (12 oz.) pitted PRUNES
- 2 cups WALNUTS or PECANS
- 4 tsp. CINNAMON
- 4 tsp. CLOVES
- 1 cup WHISKEY
- 12 oz. HONEY
- JUICE and grated PEEL of 4 ORANGES
- JUICE and grated PEEL of 4 LEMONS

Icing:
- 3 cups POWDERED SUGAR
- 1/2 tsp. VANILLA
- 2 Tbsp. MARGARINE, softened
- MILK
- Tiny DECOR CANDY SPRINKLES

In a bowl, cream together sugar, margarine, vanilla and eggs. In a separate bowl, combine flour and baking powder. Gradually blend flour mixture into creamed mixture to form dough. To make filling: In a food processor, combine fruit and nuts and grind. Add remaining ingredients and blend well. Divide dough into 3 pieces and roll each piece out on a lightly floured surface to 1/4-inch thickness; cut a straight edge on one side of each piece. Place a 1/2-inch strip of fruit filling along the cut edge and roll dough over to cover. Cut along edge with knife. Place roll seam-side down and cut diagonally into 2-inch slices. Continue with remaining dough and filling. Place rolls on an ungreased cookie sheet. Score top of each cookie. Bake at 350° for 18-20 minutes. To make icing: In a small bowl, combine powdered sugar, vanilla and margarine and blend well; add enough milk to thin as necessary. While still warm, brush cookies with icing and top with candy sprinkles. Transfer to wire racks to cool.

Chocolate Walnut Cranberry Biscotti

"There is nothing more pampering than a delicious breakfast served in beautiful surroundings. Our guests soon discover this highlight during their stay at our Inn."

Nancy Freeze—Agate Cove Inn, Mendocino

2 cups ALL-PURPOSE FLOUR
1 cup SUGAR
1/2 tsp. BAKING POWDER
1/2 tsp. BAKING SODA
1/2 tsp. SALT
1/2 tsp. CINNAMON
1/4 tsp. CLOVES
1/4 cup + 1 Tbsp. strong COFFEE, cooled
1 Tbsp. + 1 tsp. MILK
1 EGG
1 tsp. VANILLA
1 1/4 cups SEMI-SWEET CHOCOLATE CHIPS
3/4 cup chopped WALNUTS
3/4 cup choppped dried CRANBERRIES or CHERRIES

In a large bowl, combine the first seven ingredients and mix well. In a separate bowl, whisk together coffee, milk, egg and vanilla. Combine both mixtures and beat using an electric mixer until mixture is sticky, adding more coffee as needed. Turn dough out onto a well-floured surface. Knead in chocolate chips, walnuts and cranberries. Form into 1/2-inch x 3 1/2-inch flat loaves. Place on a greased and floured (or parchment-lined) cookie sheet. Bake at 350° for 20-25 minutes or until cake-like; let cool.

Note: For harder biscotti, cut baked loaves into 1/2-inch slices and arrange, cut-side down, on a cookie sheet. Bake, without turning, at 300° for 6-8 minutes; let cool.

Oldest Living Trees in the World!

Inyo National Forest is home to Great Basin Bristlecone Pine trees, among the oldest living things in the world. Some of these trees are thought to be over 4,600 years old!

Double Fudge Brownies

Ann Footer—Pleasure Point Inn Bed & Breakfast, Santa Cruz

1 1/2 cups FLOUR
1/2 tsp. BAKING SODA
1/2 tsp. SALT
2/3 cup BUTTER
1 1/2 cups SUGAR
1/4 cup WATER
1 pkg. (12 oz.) NESTLE® SEMI-SWEET CHOCOLATE MORSELS
2 tsp. VANILLA
4 EGGS
1 cup chopped NUTS (optional)

Preheat oven to 325°. In a bowl, combine flour, baking soda and salt; set aside. In a small saucepan, combine butter, sugar and water and bring to a boil, stirring frequently; remove from heat. Add chocolate morsels and vanilla and stir until chocolate has melted and mixture is smooth. Pour into a large bowl. Add eggs, one at a time, beating well after each. Gradually blend in flour mixture and then fold in nuts. Pour into a greased 13 x 9 baking pan and bake for about 50 minutes.

California's Wine Industry

The wine industry was inherited from the Franciscan monks who made the state's first wines to celebrate Mass. The Mission variety vines that the Franciscans brought from Mexico became the grape predominantly used in California. In the 1850s, well over 100 European Vinifera grape varieties were introduced. In 1856, there were 1.5 million vines and in 1858, 3.9 million. By 1862, that number reached 8 million. Although the industry was nearly wiped out by Prohibition from 1919 to 1933, today wine grapes have become one of California's leading fruit crops. Annually shipping over 400 million gallons of wine worth an estimated retail value of $9 billion, California produces 90% of American wine.

Cinnamon Baked Apples

"I find that Fuji apples have a tartness that complements the sweetness of the dried fruit and cinnamon-sugar, as well as the perfect texture for baking."

Paula Stanbridge—Windrose Inn, Jackson

4 FUJI APPLES
1 cup HEAVY CREAM
1/2 cup DRIED FRUIT*

1/2 cup SUGAR
2 tsp. CINNAMON

Core apples two-thirds of the way down from the top, leaving the bottom closed. Using a paring knife, slice the skin of the apple in the center, following the circumference, to prevent skin from cracking while baking. Pour cream into a shallow bowl. In a separate shallow bowl, combine sugar and cinnamon and mix well. Roll apples in cream, then roll in cinnamon-sugar. Set cream aside for later use. Place apples upright in a greased baking dish with high sides. Stuff apples with dried fruit. Drip 1 teaspoon of reserved cream over stuffing in each apple; sprinkle lightly with cinnamon-sugar. Add 1/2 inch of water to the bottom of the baking dish. Bake at 325° for 1 1/4 hours or until apples are soft but not mushy; let cool for 15-20 minutes. Slice apples in 1/2 vertically and place in serving bowls, sliced-side down. Spoon excess fruit stuffing on top of apples and pour a small amount of cream around each. Sprinkle with cinnamon-sugar.

*Blueberries, cranberries and/or raisins.

Apple Country

California is the nation's 4th highest apple-producing state. The industry mushroomed in the late 1800s as California's population grew following the Gold Rush, and many people turned away from toiling in gold mines to planting apple orchards. Apples are grown from Mendocino and Sonoma in the north down to Tehachapi and Julian in the south. California produces more apple varieties than any state west of the Rocky Mountains.

Date & Lemon Bread Pudding

"This bread pudding is made in the microwave and is very easy to prepare. You will receive compliments every time you make it."

Bonnie Brown—China Ranch Date Farm & Bakery, Tecopa

1/4 cup BUTTER or MARGARINE	1/3 cup chopped DATES
4 slices BREAD, cubed	1 cup MILK
2/3 cup SUGAR	3 EGGS
1 tsp. grated LEMON PEEL	1 tsp. CINNAMON
2 Tbsp. fresh LEMON JUICE	WHIPPED CREAM

In a microwave oven, melt butter. Add bread, sugar, lemon peel, lemon juice and dates and toss thoroughly. In a separate bowl, beat together milk and eggs until smooth. Pour over bread mixture and sprinkle top with cinnamon. Place casserole dish inside an 8-inch square glass baking pan. Pour 1 cup of warm water into pan so casserole dish is surrounded. Microwave, uncovered, for 10-12 minutes or until center is set. Serve with whipped cream.

Crunchy Pear Cheesecake

California Pear Advisory Board—Sacramento

3/4 cup QUICK OATS	1 carton (8 oz.) CREAM CHEESE,
1 cup FLOUR	softened
1/2 cup packed BROWN	1 EGG
SUGAR	1 tsp. VANILLA
1 tsp. CINNAMON	2 BARTLETT PEARS, peeled and
1/2 cup BUTTER	sliced
1/2 cup SUGAR	1/4 cup chopped PECANS

Preheat oven to 350°. In a small bowl, stir together oats, flour, brown sugar and cinnamon. Cut in butter until mixture resembles coarse crumbs. Press 2/3 of the oat mixture into the bottom of a greased 9-inch pie pan. Bake for 15 minutes. In a bowl, beat together sugar, cream cheese, egg and vanilla; spread over crust. Top with pear slices, remaining oat mixture and pecans. Bake for 30 minutes or until center is set. Refrigerate 2 hours before cutting.

Date Bars

Judy Higgins—Shields Date Gardens, Indio

Crumb Mixture:

1 1/2 cups QUICK OATS	1 cup BUTTER, melted
1 1/2 cups FLOUR	1/2 tsp. BAKING SODA
1 cup packed BROWN SUGAR	1/4 tsp. SALT

Filling:

1 cup SHIELDS DATE CRYSTALS®	1/2 cup SUGAR
1/2 cup WATER	2 Tbsp. LEMON JUICE

In a bowl, combine all crumb mixture ingredients together and mix well. Spread half of the mixture in bottom of a greased 8 x 8 baking pan. In a separate bowl, combine all the filling ingredients together and mix well. Cover crumb mixture with filling and top with remaining crumb mixture. Bake at 350° for 25 minutes. Cut into squares while still warm.

Shield's Date Crystals

Date Crystals® are made entirely of choice, fresh, tree-ripened dates by Shield's exclusive triple process. They resemble Grape Nuts® in appearance and are adaptable for use in many recipes.

Peanut Butter Chews

Judy Higgins—Shields Date Gardens, Indio

1 cup SHIELDS DATE CRYSTALS®
4 Tbsp. WATER
1/2 cup PEANUT BUTTER
3/4 cup POWDERED SUGAR
2 EGG WHITES

In a bowl, combine date crystals with water; let soak for 5 minutes. In a separate bowl, combine date mixture with remaining ingredients and stir until well-blended. Drop by teaspoonfuls onto a greased baking sheet. Bake at 350° for 15 minutes.

Cherry Pie

California Cherry Advisory Board—Lodi

Pie Filling:
3/4 to 1 cup SUGAR
1/3 cup FLOUR
8 cups (about 3 1/2 lbs.) pitted CALIFORNIA BING,
   ROYAL ANN or TARTARIAN CHERRIES

Pie Crusts:
2 cups FLOUR   1/3 cup + 1 Tbsp. SHORTENING
1 tsp. SALT   4-5 Tbsp. COLD WATER
1/3 cup + 1 Tbsp. BUTTER

1/4 tsp. ALMOND EXTRACT
2 Tbsp. BUTTER

In a large bowl, stir together sugar (amount depends on sweetness of cherries), flour and cherries. Set aside. To make pie crusts: Stir together flour and salt in a bowl. Cut in shortening and butter until mixture resembles coarse cornmeal. Sprinkle in cold water 1 tablespoon at a time, mixing until all flour is moistened and dough is workable. Form into a ball and chill for 1/2 hour. Divide dough in half and roll out pie crusts on a flat surface dusted with flour and sugar. Place bottom crust in a 9-inch pie plate. Add cherry mixture. Sprinkle with almond extract and dot with butter. Moisten the outer edge of bottom crust with cold water. Cover pie with the top crust, crimping edges and adding slits to vent. Sprinkle a dusting of sugar on top of crust before baking. Cut a strip of aluminum foil about 3 inches wide and cover the edge of the pie to prevent excessive browning; remove foil during the last 15 minutes of baking. Bake at 425° for 35-45 minutes or until crust is brown and juices are bubbly. Allow to cool to lukewarm before serving.

California Cherries

In the cherry orchards of the fertile San Joaquin and Santa Clara Valleys, every tree receives the ideal combination of nutrient-rich soil, sunny days and mild nights, resulting in bountiful cherry harvests.

Pecan Wine Cake

Carol Peters—Cerro Caliente Cellars, San Luis Obispo

2 cups SUGAR
2 1/2 cups packed BROWN SUGAR
1 1/2 cups UNSALTED BUTTER, softened
6 EGGS
5 1/2 cups UNBLEACHED ALL-PURPOSE FLOUR
1 tsp. MACE
1/4 tsp. SALT
2 cups CERRO CALIENTE® PINOT GRIGIO
3 cups coarsely chopped PECANS

Butter and lightly flour a 10-inch tube or bundt pan. In a medium bowl, mix the sugars together and set aside. In a large mixing bowl, beat butter using an electric mixer until soft and fluffy. Add half of the sugar mixture to the creamed butter. Increase the mixer speed and mix until smooth; set aside. In a separate bowl, beat eggs with a whisk until light and fluffy, about 5 minutes. Gradually whisk the remaining sugar mixture into the eggs. Continue whisking to a smooth, creamy consistency. Add the egg mixture to the butter mixture; whisk until smooth. In a separate bowl, mix together flour, mace and salt. Alternately add the flour mixture and the wine to the butter mixture, mixing well with a wooden spoon after each addition. Stir in pecans. Pour batter into prepared pan and place pan on a baking sheet. Bake in a 300° oven for 2-2 1/4 hours or until cake is golden brown and a knife comes out clean when inserted in center. Cool 30 minutes in pan; then invert onto a wire rack for about 15 minutes. Invert cake again so that rack imprints are showing and cool completely.

Note: For best flavor, wrap cake in plastic wrap and refrigerate for 1 day. Cake can be refrigerated up to 10 days. Do not freeze.

Finding Gold in California!

Studies have estimated that more than 50 percent of California's gold remains to be discovered!

Almond Butterwreaths

Almond Board of California—Modesto

1 cup BUTTER, softened	2 3/4 cups FLOUR
1 cup SUGAR	2 EGG YOLKS
1 tsp. grated LEMON PEEL	2 Tbsp. COCOA
2 tsp. grated ORANGE PEEL	SLICED ALMONDS
2 tsp. crushed ANISE SEEDS	CANDIED CHERRIES,
1/4 tsp. SALT	chopped
1 1/2 cups ground ALMONDS	

Chocolate Glaze:
 1 oz. SEMI-SWEET CHOCOLATE
 1 tsp. BUTTER

In a bowl, cream together butter with sugar. Beat in lemon peel, orange peel, anise and salt. Gradually mix in ground almonds, flour and egg yolks. Divide dough in half. Add cocoa to one half of dough and mix thoroughly. Shape all of the dough into narrow ropes; cut into 6-inch lengths and form into rings. Place rings on a baking sheet and decorate with almonds and cherries. Bake at 375° for 8-10 minutes or until light gold on bottom. Cool on wire racks. In a saucepan, melt chocolate and butter over low heat, stirring constantly. Drizzle over tops of light-colored wreaths and let dry.

California Almonds

According to the California Almond Board, approximately 1 billion pounds of almonds are sold annually. Of these, 285 million pounds go to American consumers. There are more than 500,000 acres of almond trees in California!

Almonds are High in Vitamin E!

According to a leading study, almonds are the leading food source of alpha-tocopherol (better known as vitamin E), the more powerful and absorbable form of the antioxidant.

KiwiBerry Shortcake

California Kiwifruit Commission—El Dorado Hills

Biscuits:
 2 cups BUTTERMILK BAKING MIX
 3 Tbsp. SUGAR
 1/2 cup MILK
5-6 CALIFORNIA KIWIFRUIT, peeled and thinly sliced
Frozen WHIPPED TOPPING, thawed
Fresh or frozen RASPBERRIES
MINT LEAVES

To make biscuits: Stir together baking mix and sugar in a bowl. Add milk and stir until soft dough forms. Place on a flat, lightly floured surface. Roll dough in flour, shape into a ball and knead 10 times. Pat to 1/2-inch thick. Cut out 5-6 biscuits with a lightly floured, 3-inch round cookie cutter. Place 2 inches apart on an ungreased cookie sheet. Bake at 450° for 9-11 minutes or until lightly browned. Cool. Drizzle a small amount of *Raspberry Sauce* on dessert plates. To assemble each shortcake, slice biscuit in half crosswise. Place bottom half of biscuit on sauce and top with several slices of kiwifruit. Dollop with whipped topping and drizzle with a small amount of *Raspberry Sauce*. Top with other half of biscuit. Dollop with a little more whipped topping and add a few more slices of kiwifruit. Garnish with raspberries and mint.

Raspberry Sauce

1 pkg. (10 oz.) frozen RED RASPBERRIES IN SYRUP, thawed
1 tsp. CORNSTARCH

In a food processor, purée raspberries. Over a saucepan, strain berries through a fine sieve, pressing with the back of a spoon. Discard seeds. Stir in cornstarch. Bring to a boil, stirring constantly, until slightly thickened. Cool; cover and chill.

A Kiwifruit's Coming of Age

Kiwifruit bloom in mid-May and are cross-pollinated by honeybees released into the fields. Kiwifruit are harvested from late September through early November.

Chocolate Roll

Carol Palluth—Oak Glen Curio Shop, Yucaipa

5 EGGS	2 (heaping) Tbsp. COCOA
3/4 cup SUGAR	1/4 tsp. BAKING POWDER
1/2 tsp. VANILLA	POWDERED SUGAR
2 (heaping) Tbsp. FLOUR	1 cup WHIPPED CREAM

Separate egg yolks and whites into two bowls. Add sugar and vanilla to egg yolks and and beat well. Then add flour, cocoa and baking powder to egg yolks and stir until thoroughly mixed. Beat egg whites until soft peaks form; fold into egg yolk mixture. Grease a 15 x 10 jelly roll pan, line it with wax paper and grease and flour surface of paper lightly. Pour batter into pan and bake at 350° for 20 minutes, until light and spongy. Remove pan and invert cake onto a towel that has been thoroughly sprinkled with powdered sugar. When cake has cooled to lukewarm, gently roll up cake and towel lengthwise. Set aside. When cake is cool, unroll carefully; remove from towel and place on a flat surface. Spread top with whipped cream. Carefully roll cake up again and place it seam-side down on a cake platter. Frost with *Chocolate Frosting.*

Chocolate Frosting

1 square (1 oz.) UNSWEETENED CHOCOLATE
1 tsp. BUTTER
1 cup sifted POWDERED SUGAR
2 Tbsp. BOILING WATER

In a double boiler over medium heat, combine chocolate and butter. When chocolate has melted, stir in powdered sugar and boiling water. Beat until smooth.

California's Chocolate Heritage

California's first two chocolate factories were opened in San Francisco by Etienne Guittard (1868) and Domingo Ghirardelli (1852). Guittard Chocolate Company, the oldest family-run chocolatier in the United States, supplies chocolate to See's Candies.

Walnut Pie

California Walnut Commission—Sacramento

Pastry:
   1 cup BUTTER
   5 Tbsp. SUGAR
   1 EGG
   2 1/4 cups FLOUR
   1/2 tsp. SALT

Filling:
   1 1/2 sticks UNSALTED BUTTER, softened
   1 1/2 cups (unpacked) BROWN SUGAR
   2 EGGS, lightly beaten
   2 cups WALNUT HALVES

1 cup UNSWEETENED CREAM, softly whipped

Preheat oven to 425°. To make pastry: Combine ingredients in a food processor and blend well. Press pastry by hand into a 9-inch pie pan and bake 12-15 minutes or until lightly browned. To make filling: Beat together butter, sugar and eggs until well-mixed. Stir in walnuts and bake 25 minutes in a 350° oven until lightly browned. Serve topped with whipped cream.

Savory Fresh Apricot Bites

California Apricot Council—San Francisco

4 oz. CREAM CHEESE, softened   1/2 cup finely chopped
12 fresh APRICOTS, halved   PISTACHIOS

Stir cream cheese until smooth; pipe or spoon into apricot halves. Sprinkle with pistachios and serve.

About Apricots

About 95% of American apricots are grown in California. Apricots are a great source of beta-carotene (vitamin A), vitamin C and lycopene. All are powerful antioxidants. They also provide iron, potassium and fiber. Apricots are low in fat, calories and sodium!

Index

Index (continued)

Index (continued)

Index (continued)

★ ★ ★ ★ *California Cook Book* ★ ★ ★ ★

California Cook Book Contributors

Agate Cove Inn, Mendocino 94
Albion River Inn, Albion 57
Biba Restaurant, Sacramento 12, 45
Butte County Hist. Society, Oroville 79
Camellia Cellars, Healdsburg 62

Capurro Marketing, Moss Landing 66, 71
Cerro Caliente Cellars, San Luis Obispo 100
Chef James Howard, Oceanside 48
China Ranch Date Farm, Tecopa 31, 97
Clarke Historical Museum, Eureka 76
Contessa Food Prod., San Pedro 38, 47
deLorimier Winery, Geyserville 50
Diamond of California, Stockton 75
Domaine Carneros, Napa 60
Dunbar House, 1880, Murphys 22, 75
Edwards Date Shoppe, Palm Springs 15
Everett Ridge Vineyards, Healdsburg 29
Ferrari-Carano Vineyards, Healdsburg 63
Fetzer Vineyards, San Rafael 84
Foppiano Vineyards, Healdsburg 61
Forest Manor B&B, Angwin 26
Grandma's Custom Baskets,
    Fresno 76, 91
Greenleaf Produce, San Francisco 37, 89
Ikedas CA Country Market, Auburn 64
Inn at the Pinnacles, Soledad 77, 93
Inn of Imagination, Napa 21
Ironstone Winery & Vineyards, Murphys 30
J. Patrick House B&B Inn, Cambria 24
Joseph Farms Cheese, Atwater 8, 44, 46
Joseph Chiriaco Inc., Chiriaco Summit 68
Lisa Edmonston, Bakersfield 80
Mäni's Bakery & Cafe, Los Angeles 85
Mariquita Farms, Watsonville 33, 36, 70, 90
MexGrocer.com, La Jolla 18, 42
Mozzarella Fresca Inc., Benicia 72
Nancy Adams, Indian Wells 73
Oak Glen Curio Shop, Yucaipa 69, 103

Peirano Estate Vineyards, Acampo 19
Pleasure Point Inn B&B, Santa Cruz 95
Real California Cheese, Modesto 7, 28, 88
Santa Nella House B&B, Guerneville 20, 56
Shields Date Gardens, Indio 81, 98
Sonoma Coast Villa Inn & Spa, Bodega 38
Stella Cadente Olive Oil Co., Boonville 35
Straus Family Creamery, Marshall 15
Sunkist Growers, Sherman Oaks 13, 74
Sutter Creek Inn, Sutter Creek 24, 92
Sutter Home Family Vineyards,
    St. Helena 70
The Philo Pottery Inn, Philo 17
Wildwood Harvest Foods, Watsonville 11,
    41, 54
Windrose Inn, Jackson 23, 96
Zacky Farms, South El Monte 41

California Marketing Groups

Almond Board, Modesto 42, 101
Apricot Council, San Francisco 104
Avocado Comm., Santa Ana 9, 27, 49,
    55, 59, 82
Cherry Advisory Board, Lodi 40, 99
Cling Peach Board, Dinuba 68
Dried Plum Board, Sacramento 14, 87
Fresh Fig Growers Assn., Fresno 34, 81
King Salmon Council, Folsom 39, 51
Kiwifruit Comm., El Dorado Hills 25, 102
Pear Adv. Brd., Sacramento 9, 36, 86,
    97
Pistachio Comm., Fresno 65
Poultry Federation, Modesto 53
Raisins Marketing Board, Fresno 32, 59
Seafood Council, Sacramento 10, 31,
    35, 43, 52
Strawberry Comm., Watsonville 40, 83
Tomato Comm., Fresno 16, 58, 78
Walnut Comm., Sacramento 10, 104

CALIFORNIA COUNTRY COOK BOOK

Easy to prepare, delicious recipes featuring fresh, wholesome ingredients—the signature of California-style cooking! Enjoy the harvest of farm fresh flavors!

5 1/2 x 8 1/2—128 pages . . . $6.95

APPLE LOVERS COOK BOOK

Celebrating America's favorite—the apple! 150 recipes for main and side dishes, appetizers, salads, breads, muffins, cakes, pies, desserts, beverages and preserves, all kitchen-tested by Shirley Munson and Jo Nelson.

5 1/2 x 8 1/2 — 120 Pages . . . $6.95

BERRY LOVERS COOK BOOK

Berrylicious recipes for enjoying these natural wonders. From *Blueberry Muffins, Strawberry Cheesecake* and *Raspberry Sticky Rolls* to *Boysenberry Mint Frosty* or *Gooseberry Crunch.* Tasty recipes that will bring raves from your friends and family. Includes berry facts and trivia.

5 1/2 x 8 1/2 — 96 Pages . . . $6.95

DATE RECIPES

Nature's candy! Enjoy the versatility of dates in these tempting recipes for breads, puddings, cakes, candies, fruitcakes, waffles, pies and a myriad of other taste treats.

5 1/2 x 8 1/2 — 128 pages . . . $6.95

PEACH LOVERS COOK BOOK

Juicy and flavorful peaches are a summer delight! Now you can make a wide variety of pies, cobblers, soups, salads and entrées with this wonderful fruit. Try *Peach Upside-Down Pancake, Peach Slushy, Salmon with Peach Ginger Salsa, Peaches & Cream Pie, Peach Ice Cream*—over 120 recipes to delight your family and friends. Includes peach tips and trivia.

5 1/2 x 8 1/2 — 96 pages . . . $6.95

BURRITO LOVERS COOK BOOK

An incredible array of tasty burrito fillings. Includes breakfast burritos, main dishes (beans, beef, pork, chicken, seafood, vegetarian) and dessert burritos.

5 1/2 x 8 1/2 — 96 pages . . . $6.95

QUICK-N-EASY MEXICAN RECIPES

More than 175 favorite Mexican recipes you can prepare in less than thirty minutes. Traditional items such as tacos, tostadas and enchiladas. Also features easy recipes for salads, soups, breads, desserts and drinks.

5 1/2 x 8 1/2—128 pages . . . $6.95

SALSA LOVERS COOK BOOK

More than 180 taste-tempting recipes for salsas that will make every meal a special event! Salsas for salads, appetizers, main dishes and desserts! Put some salsa in your life! More than 275,000 in print!

5 1/2 x 8 1/2 — 128 pages . . . $6.95

TORTILLA LOVERS COOK BOOK

From tacos to tostadas, enchiladas to nachos, every dish celebrates the tortilla! More than 100 easy to prepare, festive recipes for breakfast, lunch and dinner. Filled with Southwestern flavors!

5 1/2 x 8 1/2—112 pages . . . $6.95

VEGI-MEX
Vegetarian Mexican Recipes

Spicy, authentic vegetarian recipes. Tasty tacos, bountiful burritos, tantalizing tostadas and much more! Great Mexican foods for lacto-ovo vegetarians and vegans.

5 1/2 x 8 1/2 — 96 pages . . . $6.95

ORDER BLANK

GOLDEN WEST PUBLISHERS

☼ 4113 N. Longview Ave. • Phoenix, AZ 85014

www.goldenwestpublishers.com • **1-800-658-5830** • FAX 602-279-6901

Qty	Title	Price	Amount
	Apple Lovers Cook Book	6.95	
	Berry Lovers Cook Book	6.95	
	Burrito Lovers Cook Book	6.95	
	California Cook Book	6.95	
	California Country Cook Book	6.95	
	Citrus Lovers Cook Book	6.95	
	Cowboy Cook Book	7.95	
	Date Recipes	6.95	
	Low Fat Mexican Recipes	6.95	
	Mexican Desserts and Drinks	6.95	
	Peach Lovers Cook Book	6.95	
	Quick-Bread Cook Book	6.95	
	Quick-n-Easy Mexican Recipes	6.95	
	Recipes for a Healthy Lifestyle	6.95	
	Salsa Lovers Cook Book	6.95	
	Seafood Lovers Cook Book	6.95	
	Squash Lovers Cook Book	6.95	
	Tortilla Lovers Cook Book	6.95	
	Vegi-Mex Cook Book	6.95	
	Wholly Frijoles! The Whole Bean Cook Book	6.95	

Shipping & Handling Add: United States $4.00
Canada & Mexico $6.00—All others $13.00

☐ My Check or Money Order Enclosed

☐ MasterCard ☐ VISA

Total $ _____

(Payable in U.S. funds)

Acct. No. _____ Exp. Date _____

Signature _____

Name _____ Phone _____

Address _____

City/State/Zip _____

Call for a FREE catalog of all of our titles

7/04 **This order blank may be photocopied** CA CkBk